Food concepts by eating-designer
Marije Vogelzang

BIS Publishers

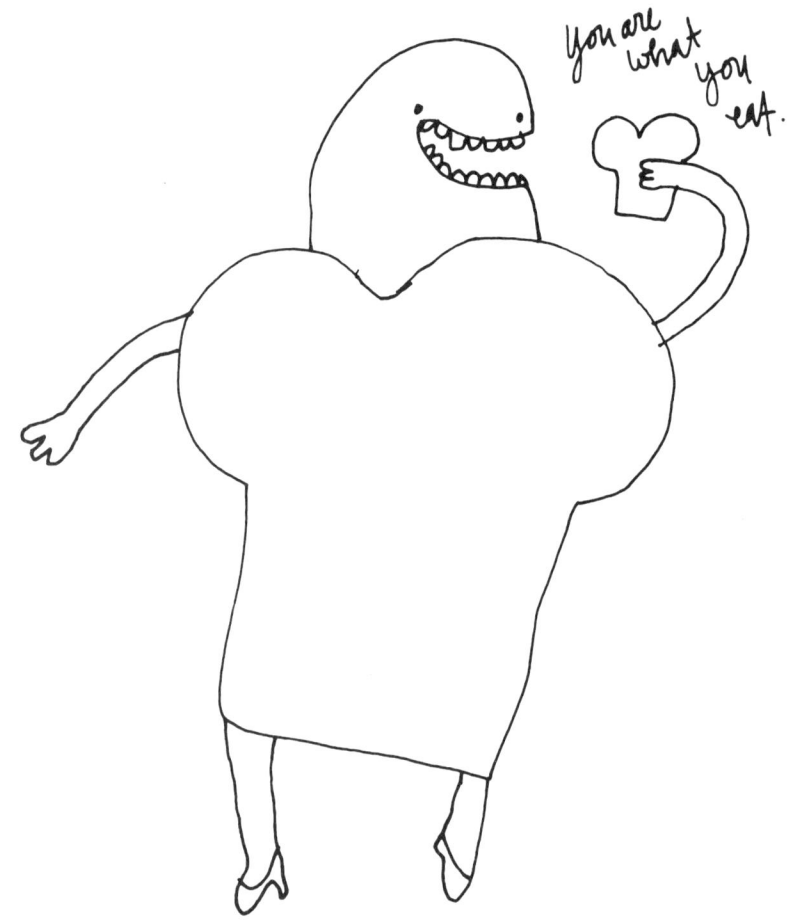

BIS Publishers
Building Het Sieraad
Postjesweg 1
1057 DT Amsterdam
The Netherlands
T +31 (0)20 5150230
F +31 (0)20 5150239
bis@bispublishers.nl
www.bispublishers.nl

ISBN 978-90-6369-200-1

Copyright © 2008, 2011 Marije Vogelzang and BIS Publishers, Amsterdam
All rights reserved. No part of this publication may be
reproduced or transmitted in any form or by any means,
electronic or mechanical, including photocopy, recording
or any information storage and retrieval system, without
permission in writing from the copyright owners.
Printed in China.

Chapters

01 Psychology   7

02 Culture   31

03 Senses   43

04 Nature   55

05 Action   71

06 Science   93

07 Technique   109

08 Society   127

Conceptual Eating design

Marije Vogelzang was born in 1978 and studied at the Design Academy Eindhoven in the late 1990s, a period in which Dutch designers were making an impression all over the world with their conceptual approach to design.[3] The same mentality could be seen from the start in Vogelzang's work. However, where her contemporaries were mainly focusing on product design, her approach to food, and everything connected with it, was based on a conceptual point of view with an aesthetic to match. The time span between the first project in 1999 and the collection of projects gathered together in this book encompasses not only a notable career, but also the development of a new field.

Very soon after graduating in 2000, Vogelzang was already much in demand as a designer for cultural events and exhibitions. Eight years later, her portfolio of assignments would include numerous companies and private individuals, as well as clients from the non-profit and cultural sector. She gives lectures all over the world about her ideas, has won various awards and has presented projects at such prestigious venues as the Museum Boijmans van Beuningen in Rotterdam, the Stadsschouwburg and the Van Gogh Museum in Amsterdam, Design fair Milan, Pioneers of change New York for Droog, the Groninger Museum, Axis Design Gallery in Tokyo, Mint Shop in London, Performa 09 New York, the Dutch embassies in Rome and Dakar, and Souk el Tayeb, the famous farmers' market in Beirut.

PSYCHOLOGY

Chapter 01

*Do you remember your first icecream?
What did you eat when you fell in love for the first time?
What did you eat when you fell in love the last time?
Why do we eat when we are not hungry?
Why do we reward our children with sweets?
Do you eat when you feel sad?
Can you actually taste it when food is made with Love?
Why do I dislike the idea of eating insects, while I do like to eat shrimps? me too!

Project
BLACK CONFETTI

Year
2005

The photographs show small, sober snacks laid out on brown cardboard trays. The location is Het Schielandshuis, Rotterdam's historical museum, where *Black Confetti* took place in 2004, an exhibition about the effects of the bombardment of Rotterdam during the Second World War. The title refers to the falling ash that, as seen through the eyes of children, fell to the ground like confetti after the German attack. Almost sixty-five years later, these same children visited the commemorative exhibition for which Marije Vogelzang and her team had prepared appropriate snacks.

The historic city centre of Rotterdam was literally wiped out during the notorious bombardment of 1940.[1] Vogelzang found it no easy matter to design something that would do justice to this traumatic time. But certainly a challenge worth taking on. Because she wanted to establish a direct link with the past she made an inventory of the few ingredients that were used for cooking at that time. What she encountered were not just negative emotions or aversion to the food, which after all was not particularly tasty. There is often an unexpected other side to disasters, fond memories can stick even to heavily charged events. Many Rotterdammers remember that they enjoyed the little that there was and how eating together created a feeling of fellowship and even moments of happiness. Vogelzang therefore decided to copy the original war recipes exactly, carefully steering a middle course between not too much and not too little.

The culinary spoilt modern citizen might feel aversion towards the frugal ingredients. But served as exclusive hors d'oeuvres, the little snacks with their references to wartime rations were enough, it seemed, to subtly affect the memory. Half a century on, a little bite of 'Valsch Vleesch' (Old Dutch for 'Fake Meat'), made from haricot beans and flour, released an amalgam of emotions, both sad ones and fond ones.

NEDERLANDSCHE VOLKSDIENST	NEDERLANDSCHE VOLKSDIENST	NEDERLANDSCHE VOLKSDIENST
CENTRALE KEUKEN **A 20ᴮ**	CENTRALE KEUKEN **A 20ᴮ**	CENTRALE KEUKEN **A 20ᴮ**
afhalen op: *Zondag 8 Mei 2005* **distributie**	afhalen op: *Zondag 8 Mei 2005* **distributie**	afhalen op: *Zondag 8 Mei 2005* **distributie**
HAPJESRANTSOEN	**HAPJESRANTSOEN**	**HAPJESRANTSOEN**
Historisch museum het ~Schielandshuis	Historisch museum het ~Schielandshuis	Historisch museum het ~Schielandshuis

Project
CUPCAKES WITH A LACK OF ATTENTION

About
Every time we make these cupcakes, I notice the psychological effect of people who decidedly choose certain messages over others, while being aware that all cupcakes taste exactly the same. Still most people will answer that they prefer flavour to visual temptation and no, they are not sensitive for textual manipulation of their choices.

Year
2001

I'm greasy, too sweet, and actually I don't taste so good

Food is not only there so that we can survive. Carefully prepared meals nourish the body and gratify the taste buds. Some food ingredients are known to have a healing effect, others are supposed to offer solace, provide energy or stimulate the libido. There exists junk food, luxury food and poor people's food. Food binds us together and food distinguishes us. Numerous religious dietary laws create solidarity among fellow believers, but also underline the differences with other religions. Food can even unleash conflicts between nations, as witness a number of 'potato' wars.[2] The world has many culinary traditions and almost every region and every section of the population has developed its own specialities over the course of time, from the pure and refined qualities of Japanese, Italian and French cooking to the complexity of Indian and Mexican cooking, for example, or the rougher tradition of the East Europeans.

Project	About
FOOD MEMORY WORKSHOP	In the context of my exhibition 'Fuel', at showroom MAMA in Rotterdam, we did a workshop with elderly people. I was curious to know their stories, memories and associations with food. Also I wanted to know their opinion about modern food culture. We prepared them some typical old Dutch (mini) dishes and collected their stories. With these stories they subsequently made edible small sculptures. One of the most frequent told stories was their complaint of children being poorly raised and having bad table manners: all… except their own grandchildren.

Year
2008

The history of eating holds a huge fascination for me; I love listening to stories from a long time ago. The world changes, but people will always keep eating, keep putting things in their mouths, tasting, remembering and telling stories about it. There are many ways to discover lost stories. Working with the elderly is one way to do it, but of course history goes back farther than a few generations. We frequently forget that there have been people living all over the world for billions of years and that all those people had to eat. If they hadn't, we wouldn't have been here!

These days we do things differently all over the world – different rituals, different ways of preparing food, different ingredients and custom – but there is also a wide range of differences in how people used to handle food in the past. In some parts of the world, food has been a means to power, a forbidden fruit, or a commodity to be traded. There are stories of competing tribes who, rather than menacing each other with spears, tried to outstrip each other by inviting their rivals to massive orgiastic feasts. Food could be an expression of wealth, a sacrifice or a forbidden temptation. Not eating is equally part of our culinary history: as part of a voluntary fast, as a method of coercion (as used on prison inmates), or in the form of starvation due to a failed harvest, war or poverty.

Looking back through the history of eating, a wealth of stories surfaces. Tales are told of the sumptuous medieval banquets held for kings, as well as stories about acclaimed wise women who could cure people with simple remedies made from onions and chamomile. There are old recipes for preparing food by boiling in clay or by canning it. Some of the most beautiful stories are about food and superstition, like the firm conviction that tomatoes were poisonous... or that eating tomatoes would drive a person mad with love. The words are fantastic all on their own: 'Lovesick Madness', I'll have a kilo to go.

One of my favourite stories is that people once believed that the roots of beanstalks grew into the earth and sucked up the souls of the dead people buried there. In the end, those souls took up residence in the beans that grew on the stalk. Eating beans brings those souls into the body – and we all know what happens when you eat lots of beans, right? It gives you gas. The farts that resulted were said to be the souls of the dead flying free again. Such a fantastic story! I love stories that have farts in them.

Even today, certain nature-worshiping traditions in Mexico bring bottles of cola and other carbonated beverages to temples as sacrificial offerings. The bubbles in the drinks ascend upwards, pointing the way to a higher plane.

Ancient tales about food can still be found all over the world. The very first recorded histories included stories about eating and cooking. It's a fundamental part of human memory. What do people do when they're homesick, away at war, or imprisoned in a concentration camp? They long for remembered flavours, fondly imagining the foods they ate at home.

I am frequently inspired by the past. It's intriguing to know that the Roman emperor Nero ate vast quantities of leeks because he thought it would improve his singing voice. Stories from more recent times can also offer lovely details. Ask your grandparents how things used to be. So much changes in just a few generations. My grandmother used to eat pistachio nuts whole, shell and all. She liked the nuts, but thought they were "a bit crunchy". It's impossible for us to even imagine a time when pistachio nuts weren't sold in shops, but my grandmother experienced pistachios as a completely new food.

I'm curious about what I'll be like as a grandmother. Will there be new discoveries then too? And what kinds of things will we see? We will probably look back pityingly at how people eat now. Maybe there will be a museum display of a microwave. My grandchild will ask me: Grandma, what is that thing? "Well, child, that was a very modern invention once, when people still had kitchens." "Kitchens? What's a kitchen?"

The history of eating holds a huge fascination for me; I love listening to stories from a long time ago. The world changes, but people will always keep eating, keep putting things in their mouths, tasting, remembering and telling stories about it. There are many ways to discover lost stories. Working with the elderly is one way to do it, but of course history goes back farther than a few generations. We frequently forget that there have been people living all over the world for billions of years and that all those people had to eat. If they hadn't, we wouldn't have been here!

These days we do things differently all over the world - different rituals, different ways of preparing food, different ingredients and custom - but there is also a wide range of differences in how people used to handle food in the past. In some parts of the world, food has been a means to power, a forbidden fruit, or a commodity to be traded. There are stories of competing tribes who, rather than menacing each other with spears, tried to outstrip each other by inviting their rivals to massive orgiastic feasts. Food could be an expression of wealth, a sacrifice or a forbidden temptation. Not eating is equally part of our culinary history: as part of a voluntary fast, as a method of coercion (as used on prison inmates), or in the form of starvation due to a failed harvest, war or poverty.

Looking back through the history of eating, a wealth of stories surfaces. Tales are told of the sumptuous medieval banquets held for kings, as well as stories about acclaimed wise women who could cure people with simple remedies made from onions and chamomile. There are old recipes for preparing food by boiling in clay or by canning it. Some of the most beautiful stories are about food and superstition, like the firm conviction that tomatoes were poisonous... or that eating tomatoes would drive a person mad with love. The words are fantastic all on their own: 'Lovesick Madness', I'll have a kilo to go.

One of my favourite stories is that people once believed that the roots of beanstalks grew into the earth and sucked up the souls of the dead people buried there. In the end, those souls took up residence in the beans that grew on the stalk. Eating beans brings those souls into the body - and we all know what happens when you eat lots of beans, right? It gives you gas. The farts that resulted were said to be the souls of the dead flying free again. Such a fantastic story; I love stories that have farts in them.

Even today, certain nature-worshiping traditions in Mexico bring bottles of cola and other carbonated beverages to temples as sacrificial offerings. The bubbles in the drinks ascend upwards, pointing the way to a higher plane.

Ancient tales about food can still be found all over the world. The very first recorded histories included stories about eating and cooking. It's a fundamental part of human memory. What do people do when they're homesick, away at war, or imprisoned in a concentration camp? They long for remembered flavours, fondly imagining the foods they ate at home.

I am frequently inspired by the past. It's intriguing to know that the Roman emperor Nero ate vast quantities of leeks because he thought it would improve his singing voice. Stories from more recent times can also offer lovely details. Ask your grandparents how things used to be. So much changes in just a few generations. My grandmother used to eat pistachio nuts whole, shell and all. She liked the nuts, but thought they were "a bit crunchy". It's impossible for us to even imagine a time when pistachio nuts weren't sold in shops, but my grandmother experienced pistachios as a completely new food.

I'm curious about what I'll be like as a grandmother. Will there be new discoveries then too? And what kinds of things will we see? We will probably look back pityingly at how people eat now. Maybe there will be a museum display of a microwave. My grandchild will ask me: Grandma, what is that thing? "Well, child, that was a very modern invention once, when people still had kitchens.". "Kitchens? What's a kitchen?".

maakt
marzepein
tijdens de
feestdagen.

Hollandse Jam in de Zak

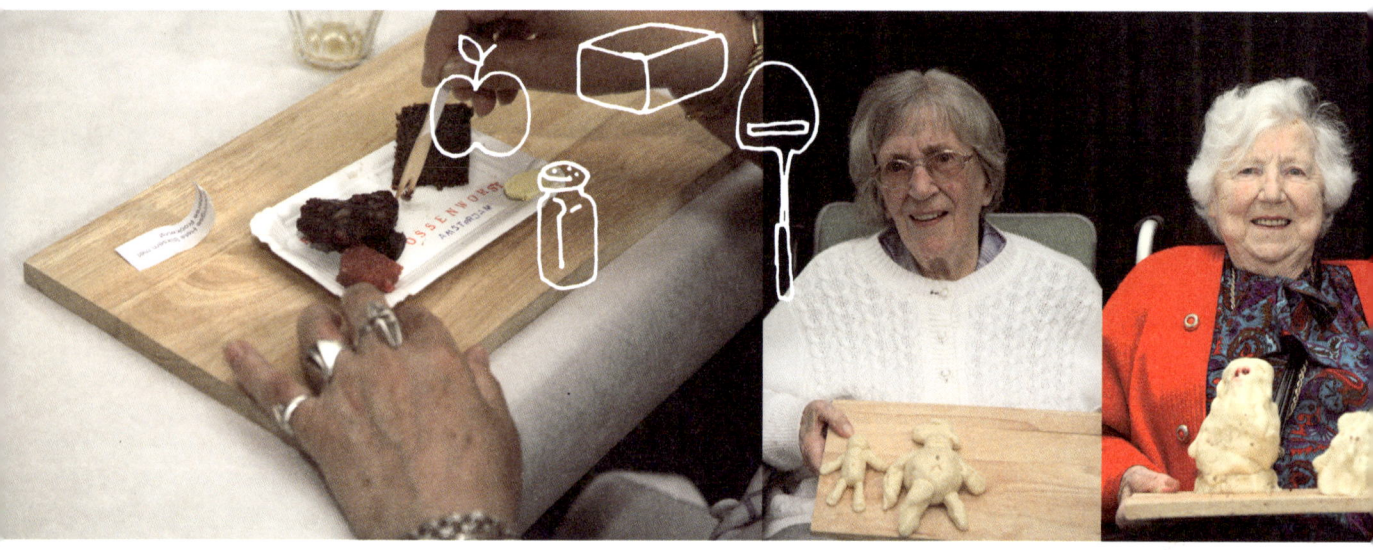

There is such abundance; just look at what children can choose from at breakfast; different cheeses, peanut butter, jams chocolate sprinkles in various flavours, crackers different kind of bread sausage, sliced meat etc. We just had bread. one kind.

Project
BREADMAN

About
Every food related issue can be tracked back to the human body.

Year
2008

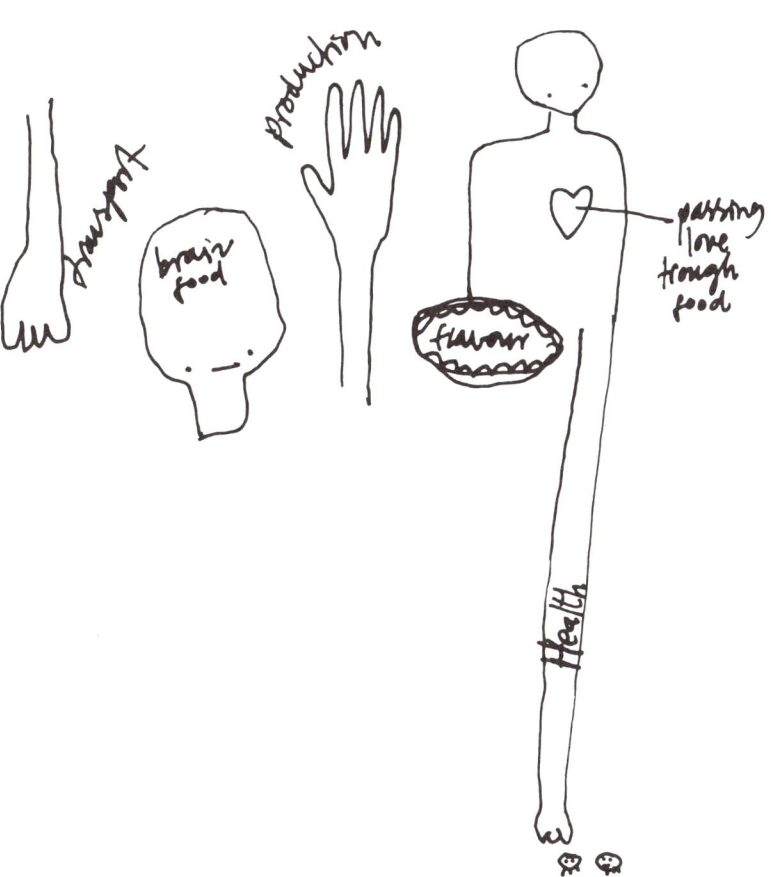

However diverse the different arts of cooking may be, tastes differ and these different tastes are usually determined by history, geography, culture and economics. The same applies to the many rituals that accompany eating. In some circles one eats according to complicated rituals and the decoratively designed attributes that go with them; in other circles the hands and simple solutions like banana leaves are sufficient. Eating is an experience to which we ascribe emotions and meanings that all too often surpass the food itself. It's not such a strange idea then, that visitors to an exhibition about the Second World War can be carried back to ostensibly buried places in their memory through food. "In fact, with *Black Confetti* it was the first time that it dawned on me that food not only nourishes the stomach but also the soul. A design can enter people literally as well as figuratively. We had obtained the original recipes from the Resistance Museum and printed them onto the trays – even that small gesture meant a lot to the visitors", says Marije Vogelzang who can be considered one of the pioneers of Eating Design.

Project
ELEMENTS

About
When entering my first restaurant, Proef Rotterdam, at the opening, guests were asked for their date of birth. According to this information we could track their astrological element: water, fire, earth or air. We then tied a coloured ribbon around their wrists, referring to the guest's personal element, and served each one of them specific food that suited best his or her own astrological element. The opening lasted a whole day. In the first two hours I noticed that there were only air and earth- guests. I started to get worried that we would run out of white and brown food and would have lots of red and green leftovers. Finally the water- and fire guests came and balanced things. Afterwards I read somewhere that water- and fire people have a tendency to be late for appointments!

Year
2005

→ with you on earth.

Project
PROEF

Year
2004

In 2001 Marije named her budding one-woman business Saai Design (Dull Design), a name that ironically referred to a preference for sober, simple dishes. When she opened her first restaurant in Rotterdam, Saai changed to Proef, which in Dutch means 'testing and experimenting in a laboratory', but also 'tasting and sampling flavours'.

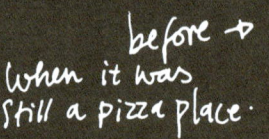

before → when it was still a pizza place.

after →

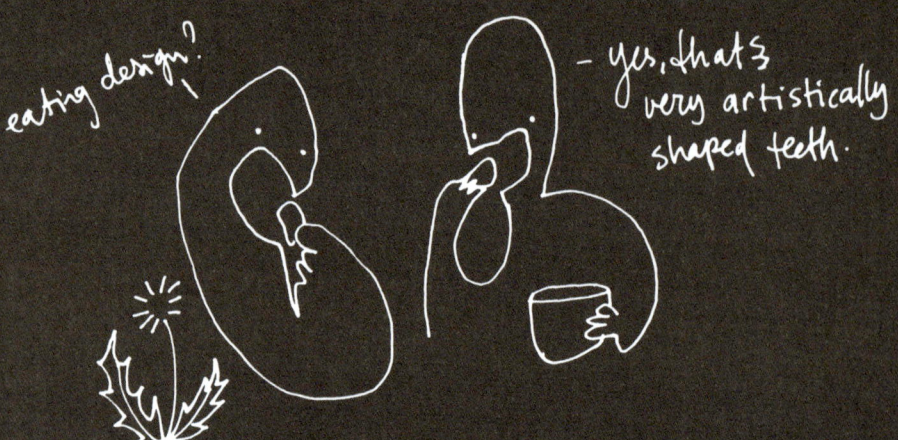

eating design?

— yes, that's very artistically shaped teeth.

Proef Rotterdam was sold in 2009; in 2010, Proef Amsterdam opened as a daily restaurant for lunch, high tea and dinner. The new restaurant is located in a former industrial building on the well-known Westergasfabriek grounds, which is home to many creative businesses. Co-initiator of both restaurants was Piet Hekker, founder of De Bakkerswinkel, which runs seven bakery shops in various cities throughout the Netherlands.

In Proef you won't experience magic or set menus; you're more likely to enjoy no-nonsense food made from good ingredients and a fun eating experience. Sharing is the central theme in Proef. What is on the menu depends on the season and what quality products are available. The delicious meat, cheeses and fresh organic vegetables come from the Lindenhoff farm in Baambrugge. Proef also has superb artisan charcuterie from Diny Schouten. The tasty pastries and desserts are made by chef Niek. Proef has 3 chickens and a rooster living over there, next to some rabbits. The veggies, edible flowers and herbs from the garden are used by the chef.

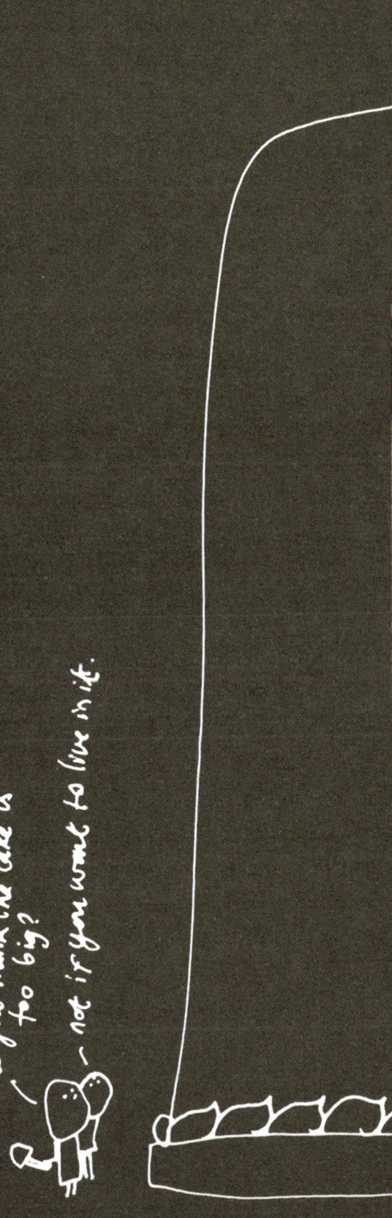

do you think the cake is too big? — not if you want to live in it.

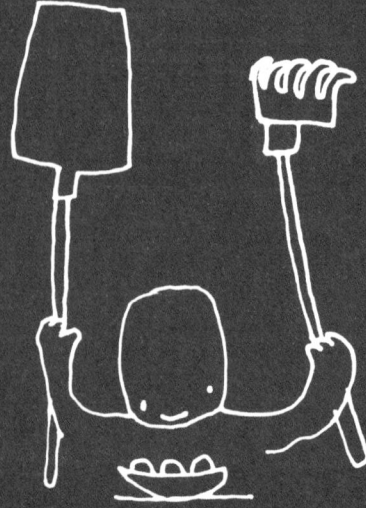

CUL
TURE

Chapter 02

* Can food bring people together?
  Can food create world peace?
  Do you know how to eat according to etiquette? Also in Asia?
  Why were women who made soups from weeds considered
  ~~witc~~ witches once upon a time?
  Do you know how to prepare a pig's head?
  Why do Dutch people eat sponge cake after a funeral?
  How can you be sure your food is Halal?
  Why do children all over the world prefer Heinz tomato Ketchup?

Project
FUNERAL DINNER

Year
1999

Vogelzang's interest in food and eating rituals was already evident during her studies. In 1999, in connection with an abstract assignment on the theme of 'white', she designed the *Funeral Dinner*. Since in many cultures white is regarded as the colour of mourning she presented modest snacks on specially designed white crockery.[4]

"White tastes turned out to be very suitable as 'solace' food. Virtually all sorts of white food taste bitter, sharp (such as celery, radish and onion), or indeed very subtle (such as cauliflower, white bread, chicken and white fish), A good combination!"

For the photo session for Interior View magazine the participants wore white clothes and were shown in front of a sober, colourless background. The result was a serene, almost rarefied and esoteric image. Life beyond life.

Back in 1999 at the academy, when I was given the assignment of doing something with the colour white, I didn't immediately think of food, but I did consider what the colour means. Many cultures see white as the colour of death. When I started researching the different funeral rituals, I saw that food plays a role in many cultures during or after the farewell to the dead. It has a certain logic for me, seeking comfort in food. Love, comfort and food are all connected, in the end. Food is the first thing a mother gives her child.

It makes it special all over again to see how we handle funerals in the Netherlands. First, black is our colour for death, and a piece of cake or a soft white roll with ham or cheese is generally all that is served, with a cup of coffee on the side. Pathetic Dutchmen!

Creating a dinner made only of ingredients that are naturally white was a logical step for me at that point. I love the idea that my kitchen is the workshop where I make things. At the academy, however, that hardly ever happened – creating a total design with food at the centre of attention. I did not opt for that choice at that time because I thought it would become an important new direction in the design world; I only did it because it seemed like fun to do something with food. It came as a complete surprise that the project attracted such widespread attention. It travelled to Milan and was published. Recoiling from the resulting popularity, my graduation product was not on food by on knitted materials.

I had not recognised its full potential. I was far too afraid that choosing food as a specialisation would make me 'the girl with the food', that I would never be able to make a table or some other 'object' again.

Even before I graduated, however, I was constantly asked to do something with food. Secretly, that was the material that I most intensely enjoyed working in. My choice to work with food was not a sudden revelation, but something that developed gradually over time. I noticed that it was the best material for me to express myself in, but I also realised that it is not solely a material to be shaped; it is far more than that. Besides a material, food is also a medium of communication. It can evoke emotions; it is connected to everything and everyone in the world. I am often reminded of something Wendell Berry said: If you eat – you're involved in agriculture.

It is curious to me that designers make everything that surrounds people – a car to take them places, a house to live in, a bed to sleep in – but that what we truly need to survive appears to be overlooked. Food is even more important than sex!

I do have to admit that a huge shift in attention has already taken place in the past 10 years, in which designers are focusing on food. But the profession is still in its early years.

Back in 1999 at the academy, when I was given the assignment of doing something with the colour white, I didn't immediately think of food, but I did consider what the colour means. Many cultures see white as the colour of death. When I started researching the different funeral rituals, I saw that food plays a role in many cultures during or after the farewell to the dead. It has a certain logic for me, seeking comfort in food. Love, comfort and food are all connected, in the end. Food is the first thing a mother gives her child.

It makes it special all over again to see how we handle funerals in the Netherlands. First, black is our colour for death, and a piece of cake or a soft white roll with ham or cheese is generally all that is served, with a cup of coffee on the side. Pathetic Dutchmen!

Creating a dinner made only of ingredients that are naturally white was a logical step for me at that point. I love the idea that my kitchen is the workshop where I make things. At the academy, however, that hardly ever happened – creating a total design with food at the centre of attention. I did not opt for that choice at that time because I thought it would become an important new direction in the design world; I only did it because it seemed like fun to do something with food. It came as a complete surprise that the project attracted such widespread attention. It travelled to Milan and was published. Recoiling from the resulting popularity, my graduation product was not on food by on knitted materials.

I had not recognised its full potential. I was far too afraid that choosing food as a specialisation would make me 'the girl with the food,' that I would never be able to make a table or some other 'object,' again.

Even before I graduated, however, I was constantly asked to do something with food. Secretly, that was the material that I most intensely enjoyed working in. My choice to work with food was not a sudden revelation, but something that developed gradually over time. I noticed that it was the best material for me to express myself in, but I also realised that it is not solely a material to be shaped; it is far more than that. Besides a material, food is also a medium of communication. It can evoke emotions; it is connected to everything and everyone in the world. I am often reminded of something Wendell Berry said: If you eat – you're involved in agriculture.

It is curious to me that designers make everything that surrounds people – a car to take them places, a house to live in, a bed to sleep in – but that what we truly need to survive appears to be overlooked. Food is even more important than sex!

I do have to admit that a huge shift in attention has already taken place in the past 10 years, in which designers are focusing on food. But the profession is still in its early years.

33

The project was repeated a few times, the last being during the Salone del Mobile in Milan where the Design Academy Eindhoven was showing works by current and former students around the theme of death and the process of mourning. "When I made the presentation at the academy it seemed to be a one-off event, especially because in the department of Man and Leisure we were mainly concerned with conceptual plans and furniture design. But my ideas for the dinner were warmly embraced by the teachers and this encouragement made me feel confident that I was on the right path. The dinner was indeed eaten but it was never served at an actual funeral. It was mainly an experiment. If you really want to organise such a dinner then it requires a different operation and different logistics. You have to be able to quickly organise something large-scale. Right now this is beyond our abilities and it is not our ambition either. But who knows, some day I would like to carry it out at a funeral. We just have to wait for a good candidate who knows the date of his death long in advance."

→ send a mail to info@proefamsterdam.nl

Project
BASICS AND ACCESSORIES

Year
2007

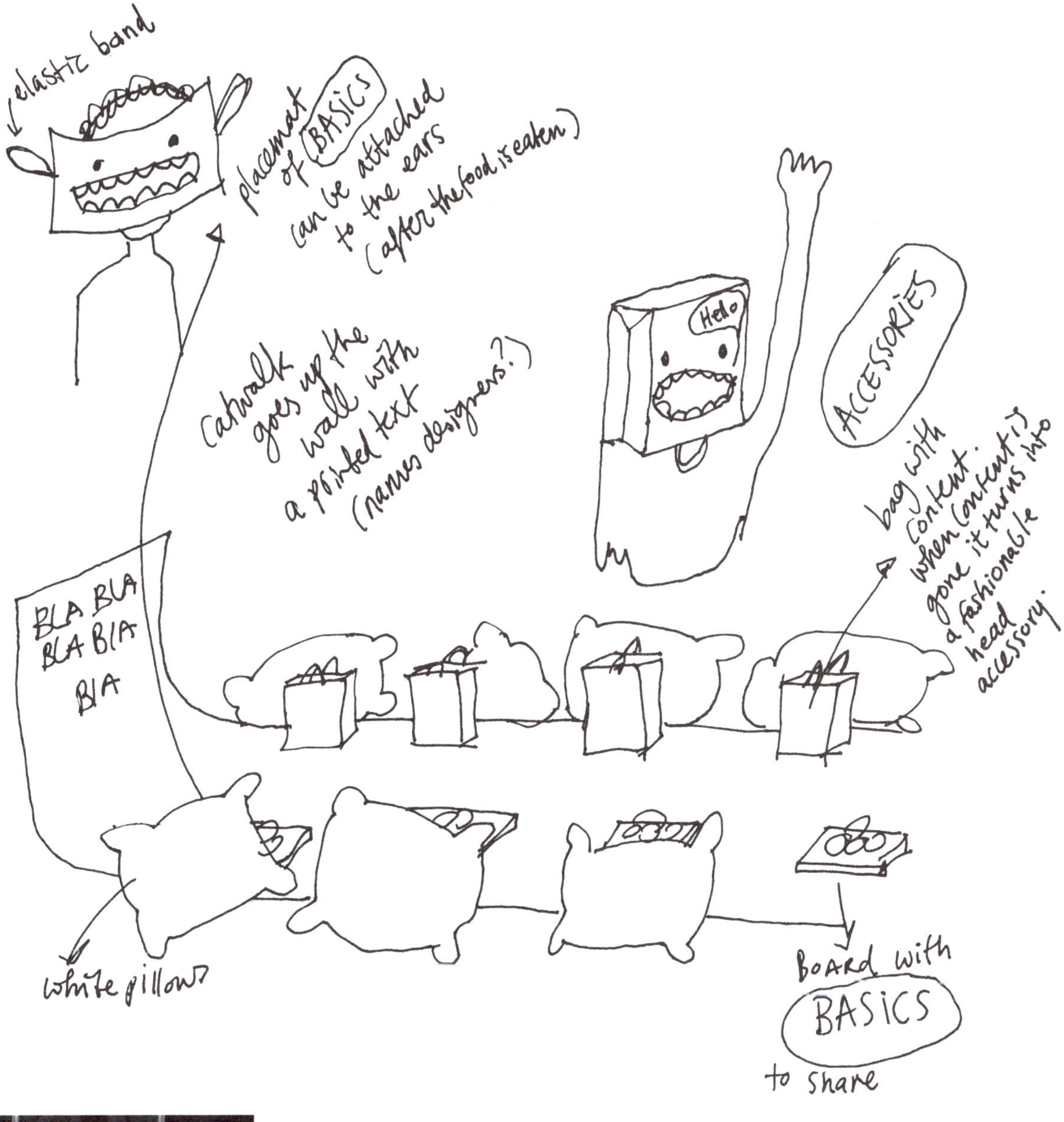

Project
POMKOMMERS

About
When I moved to Rotterdam I ate my first pom sandwich. For me, Rotterdam is inextricably linked to Surinam toko's (a toko is a little food shop).
For an exhibition in the Historical Museum I showed the map of Rotterdam and marked all the locations of toko's throughout the city. The letters on the pom-stuffed cucumbers summed up to refer to the names of different Rotterdam toko's. These names gave shape to the Rotterdam streets while the tablecloth functioned as a map. Every toko has it's own (family) pom recipe. So by eating different 'pomkommers' people could have their own Rotterdam pom tasting experience.

Year
2007

Project	About
LETTUCE ROUTE	Italy and the Netherlands have a strong history when it comes to lettuce. Dutch nurseries have been successfully trying to get the bitter taste out of lettuce since the 18th century. Nowadays bitter is still not highly regarded in Dutch food culture. The Italian food culture however is different and considers the taste of bitter as a natural counterpart for the other flavours: sweet, sour, salty and unami. Like the Netherlands, Italy (especially Rome) has a strong history when it comes to lettuce. The old Romans already used the white milky juice of lettuce because of it's morphine-like qualities. At the Dutch embassy in Rome, we made a series of simple bites based on lettuce, starting from sweet lettuce (botersla), going to peppery tasting lettuce (eikenblad and rucola) and ending with bitter lettuce (radiccio).
Year	
2007	

- smurf -
ice cream is naturally blue from dead smurfs

SEN
SES

Chapter **03**

* Why don't we use our **noses** anymore?
Does food taste different when it has a different temperature?
Why don't we like **blue tomatoes**?
Are potato-crisps still enjoyable when they sound like jelly?
Is an unglazed mug comfortable to drink from?

Project
COLOUR FOOD

Year
2002

This first food design was followed by numerous projects that succeed in stimulating the eye and the taste buds and, increasingly, the mind. Since *Funeral Dinner* went no further than a few beautiful presentations, the result was a visually attractive image of an investigation into the relationship between mourning and food. With later projects the ambition would be more to actually intervene in existing rituals and habits on the basis of socially relevant themes. A good example is *Colour Food* from 2002, a remarkable concept that Vogelzang devised for a Pediatrics Clinic in New York, where children with obesity are treated.[5]

"Offering these children healthy snacks doesn't work. They're fed up to the back teeth, so to speak, of moralistic nagging. In order to distract the children from their obsession with food their heads had to be turned."

Vogelzang therefore decided to approach eating in a different way than the usual dichotomy between healthy and unhealthy and designed snacks in the colours of the rainbow. She ascribed qualities to each colour, as described in various philosophies of colour. The red snacks, for example, were linked to self-confidence, the green to wealth, the black to discipline, while the yellow was meant to promote making friends. "It doesn't matter that much to me whether the theories are correct. The most important thing was the effect I was aiming at. I wanted to free eating from the negative associations that the children have with it. That my snacks consisted of healthy ingredients was no longer the point. Mission accomplished!"

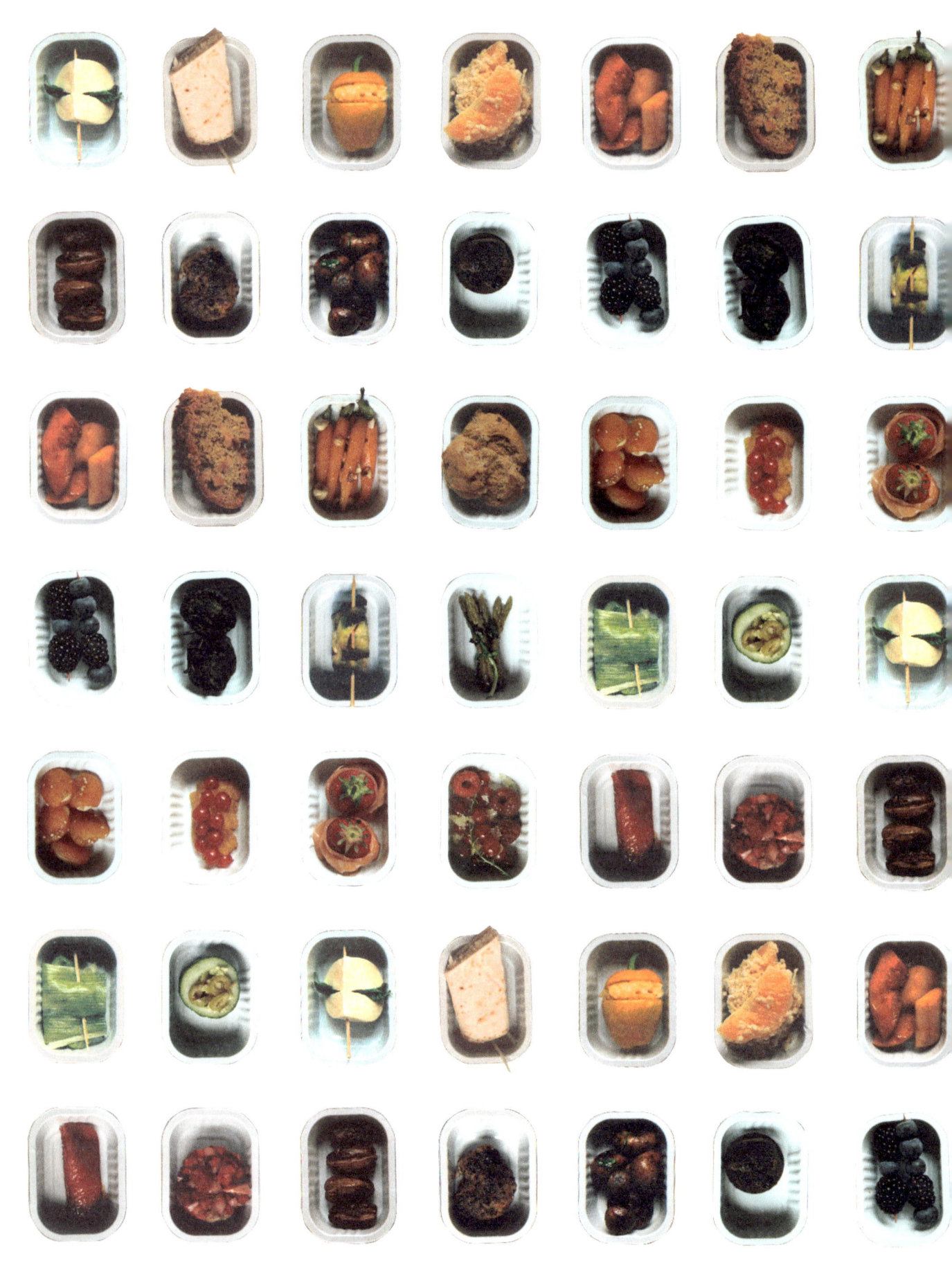

Project
EATING ON THE BEAT

About
A dish is a composition. Tastes are musical notes. Combining them and giving them space and rhythm, created a 'musical piece' in the mouth. Directed by a big drum, the guests ate little bites in a certain order. The penetrating deep sound of the drum and the feeling of having the same experience together made this project very intense and sometimes hilarious. For instance when the next drumbeat would sound while mouths were still chewing, a slight panic wave was noticeable.

Year
2007

nettle soup

drink soup

cold cucumber soup

spicy carrot soup

mozarella with lavender

roasted hazelnuts

leavened bread with lemon b...

mozarella with basil

smoked almonds

crouton met weidepâté en venkel

Working on a project, you never really know ahead of time what will happen. The project is dependent on all sorts of factors beyond your control, with no idea of how people will experience your work. Besides having a well-constructed idea, when you work with food, it is always important for the food to be fresh, hygienic, clean, and above all very delicious. No matter how great the idea is, if the food doesn't taste good, it's still a bad design. And what I make always has to be edible. I think it's a bad design if you end up with a lot of waste. In that sense, it's easier for a designer to work in non-food.

We are constantly reinventing the wheel. Even after it's been designed, we have no idea which direction the wheel will roll in. Nevertheless, it still has to start rolling before we find out if it works.

I have to say that all the projects have fairly miraculously turned out well despite it all. It's fantastic to see what can be accomplished with a team of people and to hear people's responses who experienced the work. But of course a lot has gone wrong over the years too.

Coming fresh from the academy, a designer has learned things about design, about colours and concepts. If you then have to earn your living in a field that hasn't even been invented yet, and you're also starting a restaurant at the same time, you have to try and fail a number of times before you get it right. And when is it really going well? What is the standard? Is it going well if you're earning a lot of money? Is it going well if your clients are satisfied, or if you inspire people, or if you can convey your intellectual concepts effectively? It's always a puzzle; after 10 years, I still don't have all the pieces in the right places.

But the best part about falling flat on your face is that mainly that you learn a lot; you learn so much. When we started Proef in Rotterdam, it was only four years since my graduation. In those four years, I had mainly worked alone, taken lots of odd jobs, and spent some time working with Hella Jongerius. What did I know about running a restaurant at that point? Even so, we still dived in. Exactly a month before my daughter was born, I opened the place (with my huge belly). Yeah, sure – having a baby, there was plenty of room to add that, right?

Within a year, we opened a new branch in Amsterdam. I called it an 'expansion', but it was actually just starting all over again. We spent a few more months working in a ramshackle building beside the Amsterdam location. Good thing it was summer. The butterflies flitted in through the cracks and the slightest breeze sent the bills flying right back out again.

So many things went wrong. I remember the time that we were going to cater an urban eco-breakfast in Maastricht. I drove the Proef-mobile there myself, all loaded up – that's what everyone called the company car, the Proef-mobile. Everything was stacked up in the back, including several trays of boiled eggs. Only 100 meters from the restaurant, I had to slam on the brakes for a duckling crossing the road to the park. The car braked so sharply that the eggs flew forward into the backs of our necks, me and my passenger, and hit the front windshield. It was seriously raining eggs! Most of the eggshells were cracked. (In retrospect, we were lucky they weren't raw eggs!) In the end, we cracked all the shells once we got there and served them as if it were part of the design. Creativity also means being flexible.

Working on a project, you never really know ahead of time what will happen. The project is dependent on all sorts of factors beyond your control, with no idea of how people will experience your work. Besides having a well-constructed idea, when you work with food, it is always important for the food to be fresh, hygienic, clean, and above all very delicious. No matter how great the idea is, if the food doesn't taste good, it's still a bad design. And what I make always has to be edible. I think it's a bad design if you end up with a lot of waste. In that sense, it's easier for a designer to work in non-food.

We are constantly reinventing the wheel. Even after it's been designed, we have no idea which direction the wheel will roll in. Nevertheless, it still has to start rolling before we find out if it works.

I have to say that all the projects have fairly miraculously turned out well despite it all. It's fantastic to see what can be accomplished with a team of people and to hear people's responses who experienced the work. But of course a lot has gone wrong over the years too.

Coming fresh from the academy, a designer has learned things about design, about colours and concepts. If you then have to earn your living in a field that hasn't even been invented yet, and you're also starting a restaurant at the same time, you have to try and fail a number of times before you get it right. And when is it really going well? What is the standard? Is it going well if you're earning a lot of money? Is it going well if your clients are satisfied, or if you inspire people, or if you can convey your intellectual concepts effectively? It's always a puzzle; after 10 years, I still don't have all the pieces in the right places.

But the best part about falling flat on your face is that mainly that you learn a lot; you learn so much. When we started Proef in Rotterdam, it was only four years since my graduation. In those four years, I had mainly worked alone, taken lots of odd jobs, and spent some time working with Hella Jongerius. What did I know about running a restaurant at that point? Even so, we still dived in. Exactly a month before my daughter was born, I opened the place (with my huge belly). Yeah, sure — having a baby, there was plenty of room to add that, right?

Within a year, we opened a new branch in Amsterdam. I called it an 'expansion,' but it was actually just starting all over again. We spent a few more months working in a ramshackle building beside the Amsterdam location. Good thing it was summer. The butterflies flitted in through the cracks and the slightest breeze sent the bills flying right back out again.

So many things went wrong,' I remember the time that we were going to cater an urban eco-breakfast in Maastricht. I drove the Proef-mobile there myself, all loaded up — that's what everyone called the company car, the Proef-mobile. Everything was stacked up in the back, including several trays of boiled eggs. Only 100 meters from the restaurant, I had to slam on the brakes for a duckling crossing the road to the park. The car braked so sharply that the eggs flew forward into the backs of our necks, me and my passenger, and hit the front windshield. It was seriously raining eggs! Most of the eggshells were cracked. (In retrospect, we were lucky they weren't raw eggs!) In the end, we cracked all the shells once we got there and served them as if it were part of the design. Creativity also means being flexible.

Project
HAM MAN

Year
2007

About
Inspired by the exhibition 'Barcelona 1900' in the Van Gogh Museum in Amsterdam (which focused on the art scene in of Barcelona at the beginning of the 20th century), I wanted to create a Spanish ham-tasting, using traditional high quality ham. Inspired by the idea of the 'Gesamtkunstwerk', that was popular in the 1900s, and intrigued by the sculptural quality of the work of the exhibited artists, I decided to create a ham man. My inspiration was the Dutch annual flower parade: huge sculptures, covered in flowers, are dragged through the Dutch streets like a carnival. Around 1900, Barcelona was called 'the rose of fire', therefore my 2,5 meter high figure wore 800 roses of ham each night. Building up the statue and slicing the ham in front of the audience, which subsequently could try, taste and learn about the background and qualities of the food, was part of the performance.

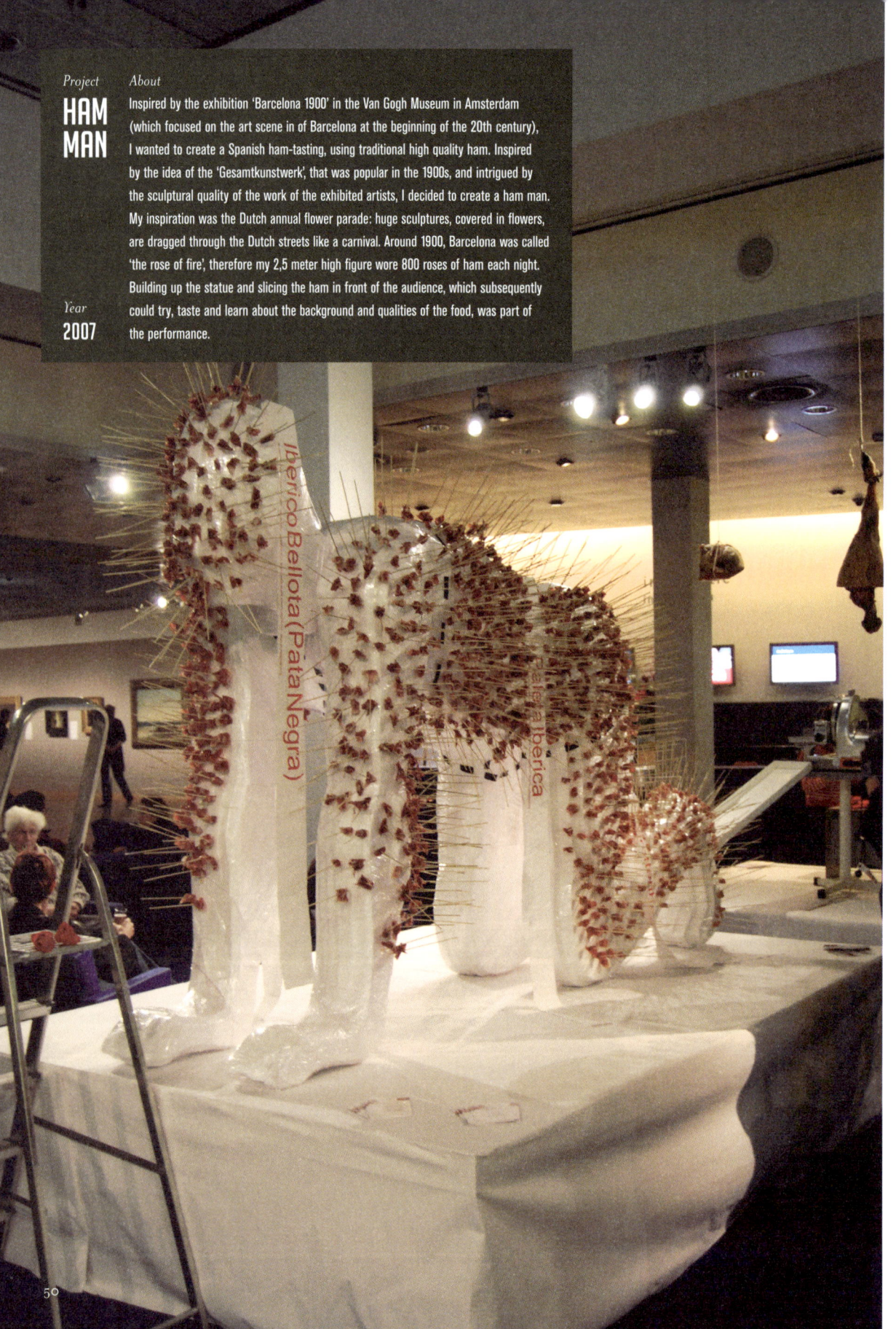

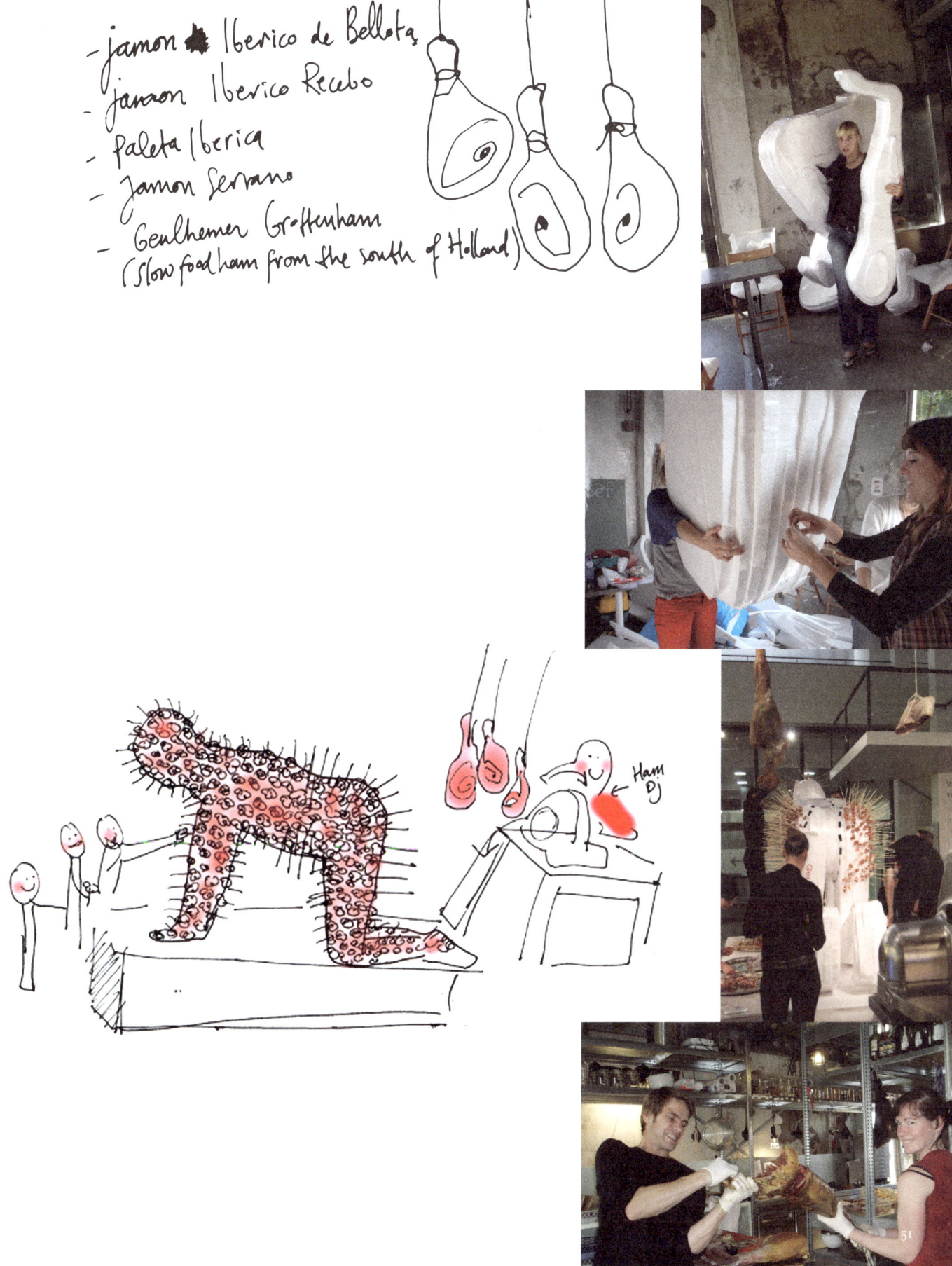

Project
FOOD WAVE

Year
2003

A greater consciousness of the ingredients in our food was the mission of *Food Wave* from 2003. Commissioned by the Artotheek in The Hague, Vogelzang designed thirty snacks that were presented in a clear arrangement on a long, specially made table. Each snack consisted of three ingredients, with one of the ingredients being replaced by another in each successive snack. Snack 1 consisted of mushroom, blue cheese, seeds. Snack 2 of bread, mushroom, blue cheese. Snack 3 of beetroot, bread, mushroom. Snack 4 of eel, beetroot, bread. Snack 5 of onion, eel, beetroot. Snack 6 of cream cheese, onion, eel. And so on. "The taste of an ingredient is largely determined by the context, by the ingredients with which it is combined. All these tastes and odours merge together and create new tastes and odours. But it can also be exciting to try and recognise the separate ingredients in the mixture." This is sometimes not that easy, as especially with complex meals tastes are so mingled that they are difficult to define separately. In that respect Italian cuisine is much more specific than many other cuisines. Instead of just throwing together different ingredients, Italian chefs dare to make sober dishes with just spaghetti, olive oil and garlic, for example. This first of all requires that the cook works with the best ingredients, and gives a lot of attention to good proportions so that none of the ingredients dominates. This attention is what you taste.

"With Food Wave I taught people to distinguish what they are actually eating, since that's a quality that we're gradually in danger of losing. And at the same time they were also able to get something nice in their stomachs."

Seed sprout leaf fruit root flower.

Why don't we make cheese of mothers milk?

NATURE

Chapter 04

* Where do ingredients come from?
Can you blame people that have survived a war for wanting strawberries in winter?
What are the differences in taste when we eat the seeds, the sprouts, the leafs, the flowers, the fruits of the same plant?
Why do children think milk comes from a factory and the forest smells of shampoo?
Why does the supermarket sell only one kind of cucumber?
Does the milk of a cow that grazes on clay soil taste different from the milk of a cow grazing on sandy soil?
Do you know when the cauliflower season in your region starts?
Can you recognize an artichoke plant?

Project
BOSSCHE BROEKJE

About
Ground layer cake for two people, which had to be cut in order to see the inside layers, representing the actual layers of soil of 'Het Bossche Broek', a nature reserve close to the Dutch city 's-Hertogenbosch, to which the title refers. The project was realised in co-operation with Helmut Smits.

Year
2007

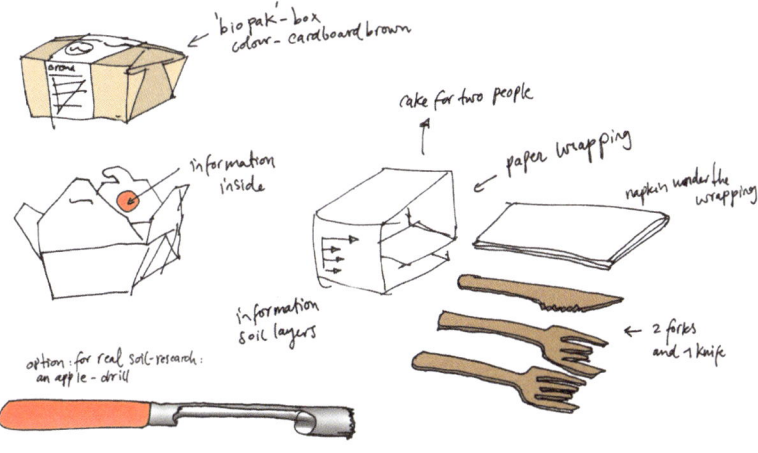

Experiencing Taste

Seeing, smelling, tasting and consciously experiencing all this - that's what Eating Design is meant to be about, according to Vogelzang. Becoming conscious is an important term. With every project a deeper meaning or poetic story can be discerned, packaged in a sober aesthetic and placed in a ritual that matches the story. It is this approach to food that distinguishes her from the culinary chefs who are usually only concerned with creating gastronomical tours de force that are then presented on lavishly decorated plates and tables. "Cooking is very popular, it's unbelievable how many new cookery books are being published and you see famous cooks working every day on television. I hardly ever watch these programmes since I'm not a cook and it's not my aim to be even more culinary than, say, Delia Smith".

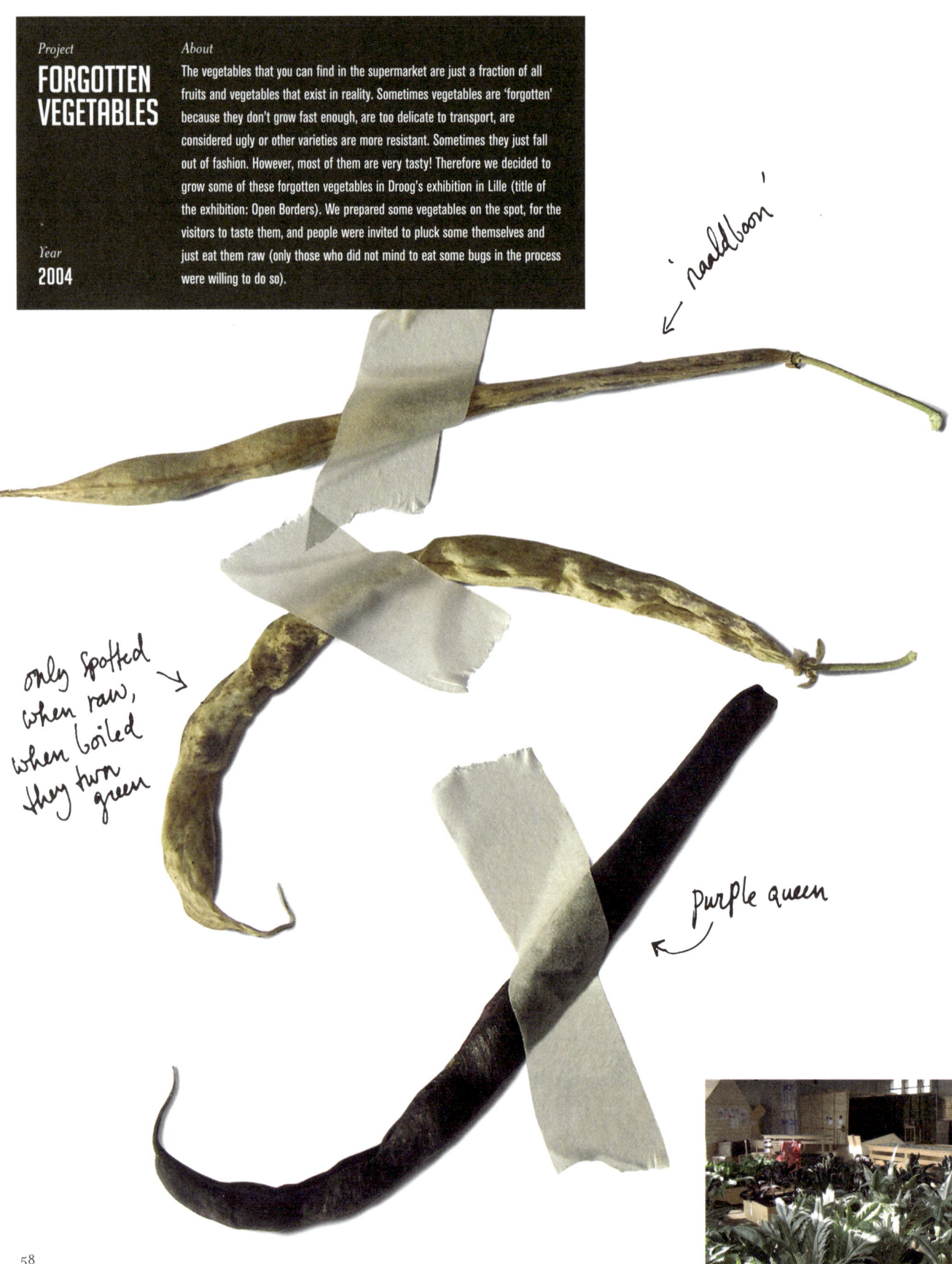

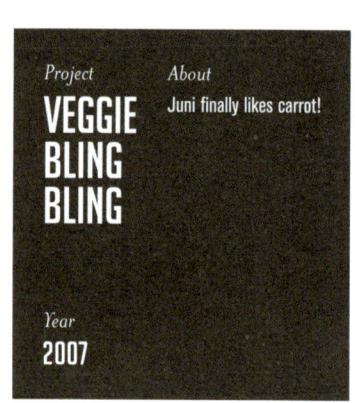

Project
VEGGIE BLING BLING

About
Juni finally likes carrot!

Year
2007

← round tools

Apple Drill

Piercings on lip or nose or eyebrow ← carrotslice with a hole

think of:
diamond ring (with a HUGHE DIAMOND)
bracelet
necklace
diadeem
earring
(also for Pirates-to be)

nibble nibble nibble
bling bling

daikon root eye patch with looking hole
eyebrow with carrot piercing
carrot earrings
carrotgreen moustache (not too deep in the nose!)
pepper necklace
pirate-teeth

end of a carrot

← nose hair

chop up all leftovers for a nibble salad and eat like a rabbit

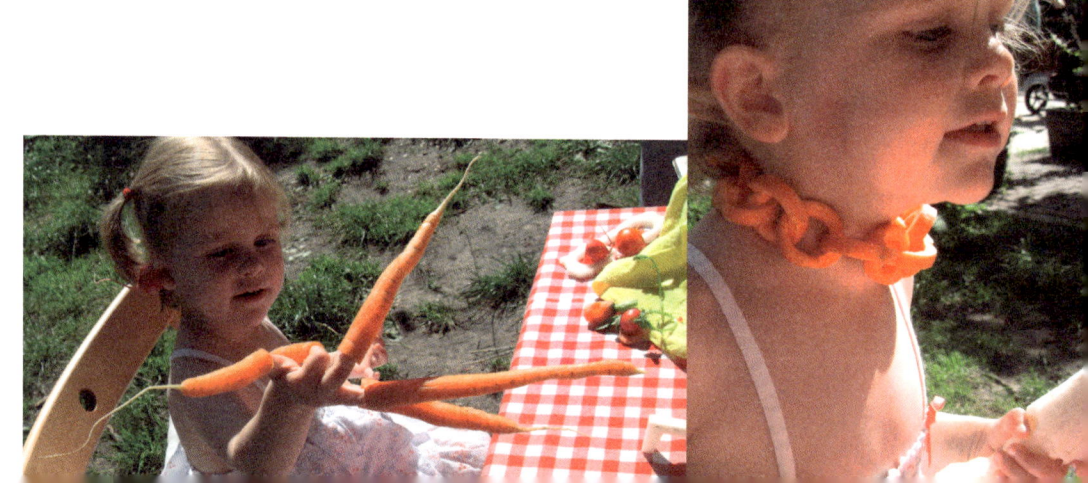

60

"I'm well aware that a business is as good as its cook. If the cook can't carry out my ideas then he or she is no use to me. I take care in selecting the cook, but that's as far as it goes." Another thing that distinguishes Vogelzang from TV chefs is the sober, almost crude aesthetic that she strives for. "For me it has to be as simple as possible, suited to the food that you're serving and the story that you want to tell.

I don't want any messing around on the square millimetre, which is often where all the attention goes in cookery programmes.

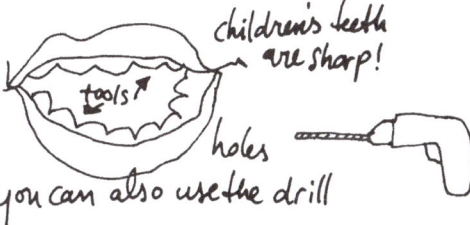

What I do like watching are programmes by people like Gordon Ramsay. There I do learn something, like how to deal efficiently with the space available and the staff. That was where I made a lot of mistakes, particularly in the beginning. Just to mention something small: at Proef in Rotterdam the coffee machine stood a long way from the till. In practice that meant an extra employee."

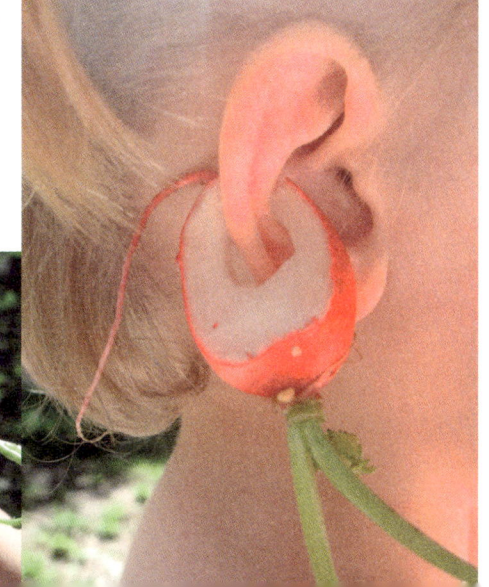

Project
ROOTS

About
Exploring the shared culinary history of British and Dutch root vegetables, I rediscovered clay cooking. Clay cooking enables one to build sculptures, bake seasoned root vegetables and create a sensory landscape. In ancient times whole animals were baked in clay on an open fire, and after being removed from the hot coals, the clay was smashed open. The cooked contents of ROOTS, in this case root vegetables, were only revealed when the clay shell was broken, creating a dilemma: breaking a sculpture to sample the warm root inside or leave the form intact. The project was an attempt to connect past and present on a modern table like an eclectic archaeological site.

Year
2008

Roots Laboratory

Vogelzang also differs from the regular catering services that often excel in extreme presentations. Increased prosperity during the last ten years has led to an enormous expansion in what there is on offer. A gigantic cake with a three-dimensional portrait of the bridal couple made of marzipan, chocolate and masses of cream? It's possible. A theatrical performance by the cook, juggling with knives and forks while preparing a fusion meal in his mobile kitchen? It's possible. Vogelzang: "I regularly have to make it clear that I don't do that. I don't make strange cakes, I don't juggle on the spot and I don't prepare exploding snacks. Sometimes people are disappointed. Because of all the attention in the press people's expectations sometimes start to live a life of their own. They're hoping for crazy things and then they find our food too ordinary. Though I do have great admiration for caterers. It's an underrated profession. If you see how much logistics are needed to make a big dinner run perfectly!"

just scoop some clay in a brown bag and make your garden happy!

and grow some root vegetables!!

The urban eco project was a few years ago; it's fun to see that foraging is in the spotlight right now. There are even Wikipedia sites about urban foraging and online maps that show which fruit trees in the city will have ripe fruit and when.

I carried out the project at various locations — which naturally also resulted in different ingredients. The things we could find in Milan were very different from what grows wild in Rotterdam. The season also played a huge role. In autumn, there are things that can be done with wild mushrooms; spring is for weeds and flowers.

I also made large scale models out of food, with the tablecloth as a city map. Laid out on the map, all the foods were stacked up in the shape of buildings at the spots where they could be found in the city.

The city. That's where most people will live in the future. A place that offers people a comfortable life, but that also increasingly makes them lose a sense of their culinary environment. We talk about children needing to learn about where food comes from, but I think many adults have no idea either. And that's not so strange, of course. Someone who lives in the city has no clue about how something is cultivated, transported or slaughtered? All those things have been shunted to the edge of the city, in industrial estates or greenhouses.

People in the city have romantic notions of a farmer's life, especially life on a nineteenth-century farm. But those romantic farms were hard work; there was no time to catch a quick lunch at a trendy sandwich shop or have a manicure after work. Besides the romanticised idea of the small-scale farmer, there is also the image of industrialised agriculture. Technology and production are seen as wrong, focused on financial profits at the expense of everything else — and at the same time, people choose the cheapest meat on the supermarket shelf.

I can imagine that children would have no idea how something is made. It's incredibly odd that an egg comes out of a chicken, isn't it? I once heard a story from a woman who told me that her daughter loved eggs, so the woman had bought her daughter a chicken as a present. Once the girl figured out where her eggs really came from, she immediately stopped eating eggs. That daughter is all grown up now and still won't eat eggs.

When I was at Procter & Gamble, I told the story of the little boy who was walking through the woods and said, "Hey, mum, the forest smells like shampoo!"

"Yes, we did that," the people at Procter & Gamble exclaimed gleefully.

The urban eco project was a few years ago; it's fun to see that foraging is in the spotlight right now. There are even Wikipedia sites about urban foraging and online maps that show which fruit trees in the city will have ripe fruit and when.

I carried out the project at various locations – which naturally also resulted in different ingredients. The things we could find in Milan were very different from what grows wild in Rotterdam. The season also played a huge role. In autumn, there are things that can be done with wild mushrooms; spring is for weeds and flowers.

I also made large scale models out of food, with the tablecloth as a city map. Laid out on the map, all the foods were stacked up in the shape of buildings at the spots where they could be found in the city.

The city. That's where most people will live in the future. A place that offers people a comfortable life, but that also increasingly makes them lose a sense of their culinary environment. We talk about children needing to learn about where food comes from, but I think many adults have no idea either. And that's not so strange, of course. Someone who lives in the city has no clue about how something is cultivated, transported or slaughtered? All those things have been shunted to the edge of the city, in industrial estates or greenhouses.

People in the city have romantic notions of a farmer's life, especially life on a nineteenth-century farm. But those romantic farms were hard work; there was no time to catch a quick lunch at a trendy sandwich shop or have a manicure after work. Besides the romanticised idea of the small-scale farmer, there is also the image of industrialised agriculture. Technology and production are seen as wrong, focused on financial profits at the expense of everything else – and at the same time, people choose the cheapest meat on the supermarket shelf.

I can imagine that children would have no idea how something is made. It's incredibly odd that an egg comes out of a chicken, isn't it? I once heard a story from a woman who told me that her daughter loved eggs, so the woman had bought her daughter a chicken as a present. Once the girl figured out where her eggs really came from, she immediately stopped eating eggs. That daughter is all grown up now and still won't eat eggs.

When I was at Procter & Gamble, I told the story of the little boy who was walking through the woods and said, "Hey, mum, the forest smells like shampoo!"

"Yes, we did that," the people at Procter & Gamble exclaimed gleefully.

Project
URBAN ECO PROJECT

About
The awareness of 'food miles' (the track food has to make before it ends on our plates) is growing. There are people that call themselves 'Locavore' and only eat food within cycling distance of their home. Maybe we can take a step further and be a 'Urbatarian'. If you walk consciously around in our urban jungle you might find more edibles than you would have thought possible. Edible weeds are growing everywhere. Pigeons fly on every square. Many parks, graveyards and flowerbeds reveal edible nuts, berries or mushrooms. There are ducks in the pond and they also lay eggs. All this is not 'produced'. It's just there; you might even tramp on it while walking to your office or workplace.

Year
2004

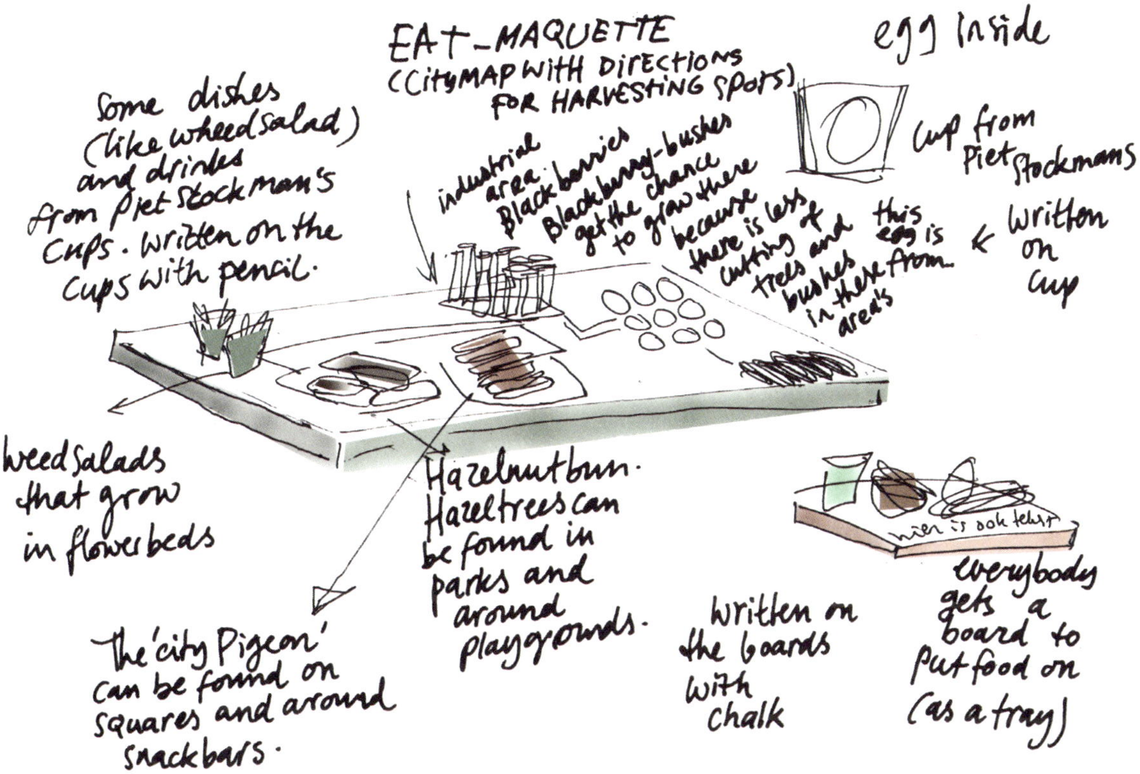

EAT_MAQUETTE
(CITYMAP WITH DIRECTIONS FOR HARVESTING SPOTS)

egg inside

Some dishes (like weed salad) and drinks from Piet Stockman's cups. Written on the cups with pencil.

industrial area

Blackberry-bushes get the chance to grow there because there is less cutting of trees and bushes in there areas

cup from Piet Stockmans

this egg is written on cup

weed salads that grow in flower beds

Hazelnut bun. Hazeltrees can be found in parks and around playgrounds.

The 'city Pigeon' can be found on squares and around snackbars.

written on the boards with chalk

everybody gets a board to put food on (as a tray)

dandelion pancakes.

dandelion comes from 'dents de lion' which means 'lion teeth' referring to the shape of the leafs. But in french dandelion is called 'pisselit' which means 'piss in your bed' because eating dandelion leafs make you go to the toilet.

Wild → Dutch people are not used to eating pigeon. Some visitors were a bit suspicious but tried our grilled pigeons anyway and found that they are actually very tasty.

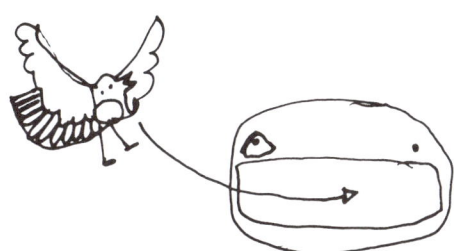

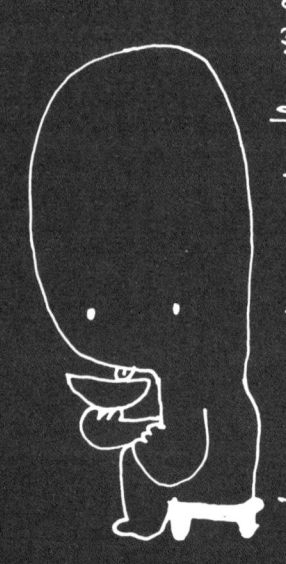

Licking soup like a cat is the new dietary fashion.

ACT
ION

Chapter
05

* When was the last time that someone fed you?
In how many ways can you share food?
What is the best room temperature for eating Gazpacho? Sauerkraut?
Did the ancient Romans have a good reason for lying down when eating?
Did you ever eat sitting on a swing?
What is the maximum size that a spoon can be?
Did you ever try to eat without your hands?
With whom will you end up fighting when cooking together?

Project
DISTANCE LUNCH

About
Eating in the Show-Room: cutlery dictates both the body language and the distance to the food.

Year
2006

While the difference from both chefs and the regular catering circuit is clear, there is also an important difference from Food Designers. "I was not the first designer to be involved with food. But I soon noticed that most designers were almost exclusively concentrating on the presentation, the styling of the food. The aesthetic aspect is very important, I think - as far as that goes I'm a real designer. But it has to do more than that. You can see that in the photographs which in the end are the only things that remain of all these short-lived projects. The photographs show that I design not only the food but also the experience that goes with it, the actions."[6]

Because I'm not just focussed on the aesthetics, I deliberately don't call myself a Food Designer but an Eating Designer. The food itself is already perfectly designed by nature, so there's hardly anything I have to add to it.

Eating is a more active concept, a verb. You could say I'm concerned with everything that plays an active role when it comes to food: growing, harvesting, washing, cutting, preparing, tempting, serving, eating… The profession was in its infancy when I began and this gave me a lot of freedom to develop my own ideas." Ilse Crawford, English magazine editor and design consultant: "Food inevitably affects the taste buds. But Marije's food projects affect your whole being, even on a subliminal level. She creates total experiences. What's more, she's a great person to work with and that's visible in the end result."

Project
SHARING DINNER

Year
2005

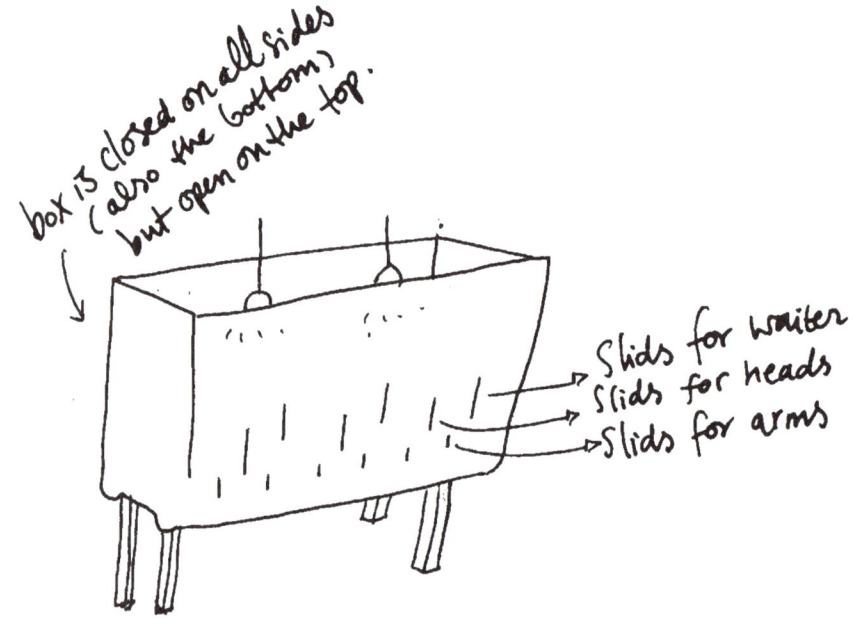

One example of food as a total experience is *Sharing Dinner* from 2005. "When Droog asked me to design a Christmas dinner I hesitated at first. Christmas dinners are usually over-designed, over-decorated and laden with rituals and clichés. But when I looked more deeply into the subject I realised that Christmas is not at all about the turkey and the Christmas biscuits. Besides the religious aspect it's about sharing and togetherness." Vogelzang therefore decided to focus on the communication between people and to limit the food to the familiar classics that are anchored in the collective memory, such as ham with melon for starters and rib for the main course. The table was covered by a large tablecloth whose edges were suspended from the ceiling. The guests were invited to stick their head and hands through special openings in the cloth. People could thus no longer be distinguished by their clothes, a wink to both the Christian tradition and Communist ideals of equality. The guests were then seduced in various ways to make contact with each other. The starter was served

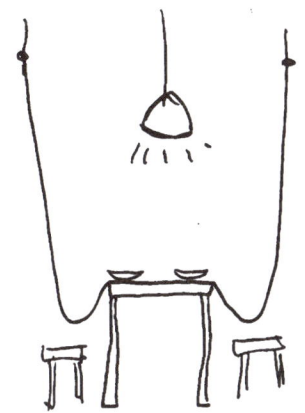 

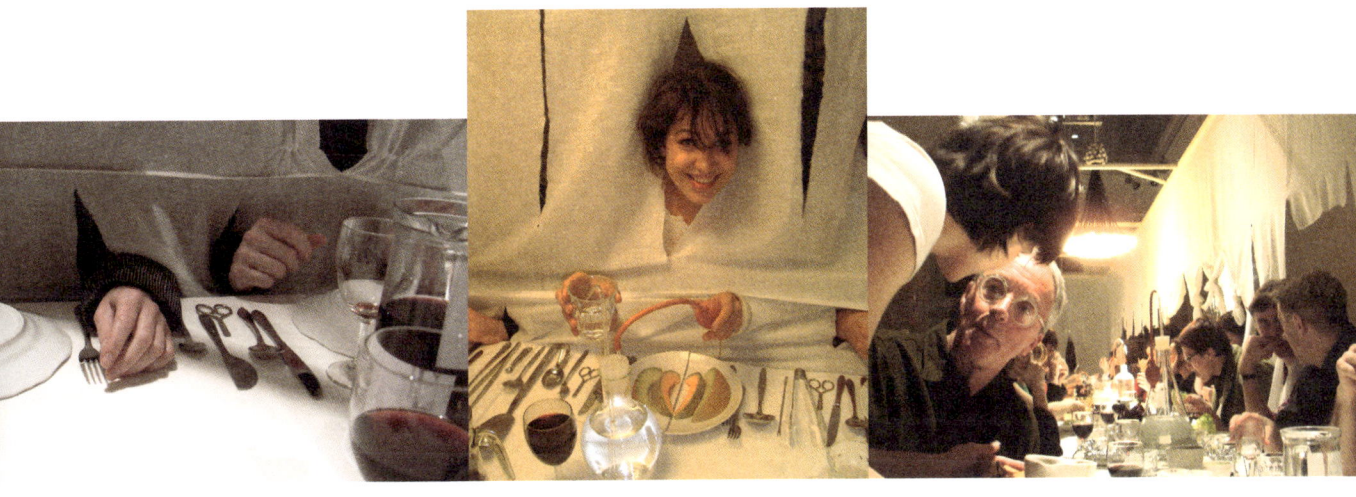

on plates sawn through the middle and containing only the ham or only the melon, so that neighbours had to swap dishes. With the main course the one guest was served an entire head of lettuce and the others a whole rib, the potatoes or just the gravy. In order to dine completely they had to share the food with each other. "I was a bit worried whether people would cooperate, as most of the people didn't know each other. But there immediately arose an animated and even hilarious atmosphere, as when someone had to go to the toilet, for example, and asked another person to hold the champagne glass, which was attached to the other glasses with a ribbon, for a moment. It was only after the second course that people started getting mischievous, cutting away the tablecloth with the pair of scissors that I had placed with the cutlery. My concept was not meant to become a straitjacket. The liberation of the tablecloth was something that I'd built in in advance. Designed. All in all it was a very successful gathering. A genuine Christmas dinner!"

Gijs Bakker, co-director of Droog and one of Vogelzang's clients from the very beginning: "What Marije adds is a sensitivity to the context. She is unbelievably good at listening and analysing. Whenever she gets a commission she comes and talks extensively about all the ins and outs of the situation. Cooks and catering companies concentrate almost exclusively on the food and hardly take into account the people for whom it is being made. And most designers only pay attention to beautiful styling." Vogelzang: "When I'm asked for a special event then I go deeply into the subject and only gradually think up which food will suit that. At the same time I also think about how the food should be presented, by whom, what they are wearing and what they will say. Everything counts - where the ingredients come from, the taste, the smell, the texture, the vitamins, the sound made by eating, the cultural meanings that are attached, the emotional value, the way in which it is eaten. Not all these elements are used in every project but in principle I take everything into consideration. The moment you engross yourself in the profession you very soon notice that people work with the same standard meals and preparations, regardless of the context. There might well be all sorts of additions, like theatre or dance, but these extras are usually just standard solutions."

Project
BUTTERFLIES

About
The weight of the bites on the long rods makes the installation 'bounce' like a swarm of butterflies.

I think the most exceptional thing about working with food is that my work allows me to 'crawl inside someone's skin'. People often ask me if I mind that my work is demolished and consumed. In my view, though, the design is not finished when the food is set on the table (if there's a table), but when it is in the stomach of the person for whom the food was made. Or maybe when that person takes it along to the toilet. The experience of the person eating is also part of the design.

It's fantastic that my work ultimately disappears down the toilet. Essentially, I just make a kind of interestingly packaged poop. It's a liberating idea. Maybe that's why most designers want to work with 'permanent' materials. They want to earn immortality for themselves through the material that will outlive them. That's fine, but let me make poop. That's why I don't see the aesthetics of design and styling as an end in themselves but as a tool to achieve the ultimate goal: communication.

Sometimes I communicate about food miles or the psychology of eating, about education or culture. No one will be persuaded to listen to a story just by shouting the story at them. If you want someone to listen, you have to package your story well, make it tasty. That's the function of aesthetics in my work. I don't make something because it looks nice. If it looks pretty, that's because it serves to support the experience that the eater will have. I have noticed that my interest in making a shape is ebbing away and that I am increasingly more interested in the creative conceptual process than in the result itself. I sometimes wonder whether I want to keep calling myself a designer. I do come from a design background, but sometimes I think the word 'design' is not free enough.

So what should I call myself then?
Culinary thinker? Food philosopher?
Creative food fiddler?
Maybe I need some help to figure this out. If you have a suggestion, let me know! Email your idea to studio@marijevogelzang.nl; the winner will receive nicely packaged poop!

I think the most exceptional thing about working with food is that my work allows me to 'crawl inside someone's skin'. People often ask me if I mind that my work is demolished and consumed. In my view, though, the design is not finished when the food is set on the table (if there's a table), but when it is in the stomach of the person for whom the food was made. Or maybe when that person takes it along to the toilet. The experience of the person eating is also part of the design.

It's fantastic that my work ultimately disappears down the toilet. Essentially, I just make a kind of interestingly packaged poop. It's a liberating idea. Maybe that's why most designers want to work with 'permanent' materials. They want to earn immortality for themselves through the material that will outlive them. That's fine, but let me make poop. That's why I don't see the aesthetics of design and styling as an end in themselves but as a tool to achieve the ultimate goal: communication.

Sometimes I communicate about food miles or the psychology of eating, about education or culture. No one will be persuaded to listen to a story just by shouting the story at them. If you want someone to listen, you have to package your story well, make it tasty. That's the function of aesthetics in my work. I don't make something because it looks nice. If it looks pretty, that's because it serves to support the experience that the eater will have. I have noticed that my interest in making a shape is ebbing away and that I am increasingly more interested in the creative conceptual process than in the result itself. I sometimes wonder whether I want to keep calling myself a designer. I do come from a design background, but sometimes I think the word 'design' is not free enough.

So what should I call myself then? Culinary thinker? Food philosopher? Creative food fiddler? Maybe I need some help to figure this out. If you have a suggestion, let me know! Email your idea to studio@marijevogelzang.nl; the winner will receive nicely packaged poop!

the weight of the snack makes the installation 'bounce'

Project
RUIS

About
The lamps kept the food warm and provided the only light in the space. Underneath the lamps was a long food table, surrounded by chairs for the visitors. Starting with a virgin white edible landscape the eaters created 'ruis' (noise) by digging up curries with different colours and flavours.

Year
2005

Project
BITS AND BYTES

Year
2010

About
Bits and Bytes is (b)all about communication and serves uncommon but truly delicious food, all in ball sizes. It is an installation of white trays filled with marble-like sweets; called magic balls in Dutch, they look like gumballs and have several layers of different colours. When you eat them, they change color! The food is placed in bowls and moves forward on the balls like a (low tech) conveyor belt. Guests are encouraged to push the plates of food forward to help each other. In front of the trays with balls, every guest has his or her own small plate to put their food on. Guests can add small notes and send them to someone they know across the table, just by rolling the balls.

Project
BURNS NIGHT SUPPER

About
Traditional Scottish peasant food made in a contemporary way.

Year
2008

in the middle of the table
lots of different dishes
made from root vegetables
and vegetarian haggis
all served in a mix of teacups

- glazed purple carrot
- marinated yellow beetroot
- grilled jerusalem artichoke with hazelnuts

Puffed beetroot with balsamic vinegar

vegetarian haggis

turnip parsnip-chips with pepper and seasalt

- black salsify
- haggis made of highland beef.

Project
BALLS

SCIENCE

Chapter 06

※ What happens when food enters your body?
How was mayonnaise discovered?
Why do I get scared when I read about genetically created meat (not modified, created), also known as in vitro meat, or meat made of stem cells of animals?
Does 'in vitro meat' have a soul?
Can food be used as a medicine?
Why don't they serve more carrots in the hospital's eye ward?
Could eating lots of carrots make you look orange?
Why did we develop more food allergies over the past decades?
What do vitamins look like?

Project
DUTCH NATIONAL TAPWATER TASTING

Year
2007

About
Dutch water from the tap is one of the purest waters in the world. We drink it but also flush our toilets with it. The water comes from various sources in different places. When traveling through Holland I always notice the differences in taste of tap water. We brought together 12 waters from the capitals of the 12 Dutch provinces (yes, somebody actually drove a van across the country!). It was a unique moment because normally you don't find these different waters together at one spot. The 130 glass liter-bottles per capital gave immediate insight into the amount of water that is used daily by an average Dutch person: 130 liter (for drinking, showering, laundry, toilet etc.).

De Nationale kraanwater proeverij

Van 14 oktober t/m 4 november 2007 kunt u elke zondag bepalen welke provincie in Nederland het lekkerste kraanwater heeft.

Een project van Marije Vogelzang in samenwerking met Liesje Diemont

lokatie: Rioolgemaal Moerenburg
Hoevense kanaaldijk 38
5018 TE Tilburg
open iedere zondag
van 14:00 tot 17:00
06-5339497

www.tilburg.nl/kort

Dit project is ontstaan in het kader van broedplaats Moerenburg, een samenwerking tussen Kort, Gemeente Tilburg afdeling cultuur en theater De NWE vorst. Het project is mede mogelijk gemaakt door de afdeling economie van de gemeente Tilburg.

Kort (kunst in de openbare ruimte Tilburg) is een samenwerkingsverband tussen de gemeente Tilburg en de NBKS (Nieuwe Brabantse Kunst Stichting)

Typical 'Brabantse' bar
Customer 1: Well, that's certainly the best water I've ever drunk!
Customer 2: yeah!

I can really get wrapped up in reading about human behaviour studies — especially in relation to food, obviously. Quite a lot of scientific research is conducted in the world of food. That research is in high demand, or is funded by the food industry or by marketers. Studies have been done on how people assess the taste of wine in different packages; an average vintage in a bottle with a high price and a fancy name is generally considered much more delicious than the same wine in a bottle labelled as the house brand. And research has been conducted on eating behaviour depending on whether or not there is any trace of what the person is eating; as it turns out, people eat significantly less when the bones of the chicken wings are left on the table in plain sight, compared to when the bones are cleared away immediately. Findings like this intrigue me immensely.

When I was a little girl and we had visitors, I loved making the snacks. Of course I enjoyed making something in the kitchen and arranging it nicely on a little plate. With a flower on it. But the main thing I remember is that I wanted to serve the snacks myself to see how people responded. Sometimes I had decorated each cracker just a little differently, or sliced some pieces of sausage just a bit thicker than others, or arranged meatballs with and without a cocktail stick, and so on. Nothing fancy, right? It was the 80s, after all. Hors d'oeuvres at our house were just crackers with liverwurst and a drop of ketchup on top. Looking back, I would have to say that my interest in human behaviour must have started then, on a very small scale.

Proef isn't called Proef for nothing. It means tasting, but it also means testing. I am still extremely fascinated to watch what happens when people are surprised with specific foods in certain situations. Especially where food is concerned, people turn out to be strong creatures of habit.

When we just started working in Amsterdam, I had the brilliant idea that it could be interesting to come up with a different culinary concept every six weeks. Complete with a new menu, a new décor, different uniforms for the serving staff and a different 'performance'. I actually thought it would be a good idea, haha!

We enthusiastically started out that way, taking on the task of rigorously changing everything every six weeks. What happened was that people ate there once and then came back again a few weeks later. They didn't understand it at all; they thought that the restaurant had been sold to someone else and were disappointed. These patrons were coming back precisely because they had really enjoyed something they ate the first time. They didn't want a new concept at all – no matter how fun the new concept was. There's a difference here between a restaurant and catering. In catering, people do want to have something new. At a restaurant, in contrast, they would rather come back again to have that thing that was so delicious last time. Boring, isn't it? I do it too.

*These are two examples from 'mindless eating' by Brian Wansink

I can really get wrapped up in reading about human behaviour studies — especially in relation to food, obviously. Quite a lot of scientific research is conducted in the world of food. That research is in high demand, or is funded by the food industry or by marketers. Studies have been done on how people assess the taste of wine in different packages; an average vintage in a bottle with a high price and a fancy name is generally considered much more delicious than the same wine in a bottle labelled as the house brand. And research has been conducted on eating behaviour, depending on whether or not there is any trace of what the person is eating; as it turns out, people eat significantly less when the bones of the chicken wings are left on the table in plain sight, compared to when the bones are cleared away immediately. Findings like this intrigue me immensely.

When I was a little girl and we had visitors, I loved making the snacks. Of course I enjoyed making something in the kitchen and arranging it nicely on a little plate. With a flower on it. But the main thing I remember is that I wanted to serve the snacks myself to see how people responded. Sometimes I had decorated each cracker just a little differently, or sliced some pieces of sausage just a bit thicker than others, or arranged meatballs with and without a cocktail stick, and so on. Nothing fancy, right? It was the 80s, after all. Hors d'oeuvres at our house were just crackers with liverwurst and a drop of ketchup on top. Looking back, I would have to say that my interest in human behaviour must have started then, on a very small scale.

Proef isn't called Proef for nothing. It means tasting, but it also means testing. I am still extremely fascinated to watch what happens when people are surprised with specific foods in certain situations. Especially where food is concerned, people turn out to be strong creatures of habit.

When we just started working in Amsterdam, I had the brilliant idea that it could be interesting to come up with a different culinary concept every six weeks. Complete with a new menu, a new décor, different uniforms for the serving staff and a different 'performance'. I actually thought it would be a good idea, haha!

We enthusiastically started out that way, taking on the task of rigorously changing everything every six weeks. What happened was that people ate there once and then came back again a few weeks later. They didn't understand it at all; they thought that the restaurant had been sold to someone else and were disappointed. These patrons were coming back precisely because they had really enjoyed something they ate the first time. They didn't want a new concept at all – no matter how fun the new concept was. There's a difference here between a restaurant and catering. In catering, people do want to have something new. At a restaurant, in contrast, they would rather come back again to have that thing that was so delicious last time. Boring, isn't it? I do it too.

*These are two examples from 'mindless eating', by Brian Wansink

Happy family from Leeuwarden
Father: When we go on holiday to France we always drive via Venray for a bottle of Venray's water. We all love it.
Mother: Especially as in France we can't get used to the taste of chlorine.

A bar in Amsterdam
Customer 1: You can say that again, but give me an Amsterdam municipal beer!
Customer 2: What did you say?

memory - pumpkin, ginger
Sex - artichoke cashew nuts
Supleness - olives

concentration - spinach feta
energy - goatcheese figs
youth - tuna anchois
vitality - eel pineseeds
brains - onion sage
kick - schrimp dill

asking what visitors would need; energy, concentration or perhaps →or want
Sex, made people give quite honest answers. A bit dissapointing
was that most women chose to have youth, while the majority of
men ordered Sex-peppers.

Project
PHOTOSYNTHESISTREE

Year
2008

About
Two of the basic scientific principles are gravity and photosynthesis. Photosynthesis is the process by which green plant leaves absorb sunlight and transfer it into energy and food. The Photosynthesistree combines these two principles. The tree produces food, leaf-shaped biscuits, by harnessing the energy and light from desk lamps. The heat from the lamps functions as a 'stove' to bake the dough leaves, which are ready when they become crunchy and golden brown and fall to the ground like autumn leafs.

When I showed this installation to the elderly people at page 16 one of the ladies commented: But why don't you just use a pan?

ehm, yes...

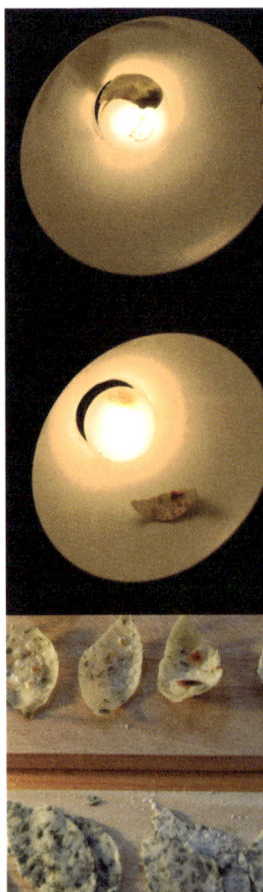

Project

ENERGY- AND RELAX MENU

Year
2006

About

Dietary science has written heaps of books about the effect of food on the body. Using this information I made an energy- and a relax menu. Guests could decide if they needed to wake up or wind down. We provided a stamp on the hand with an energizing or a relaxing scent. All the food was balanced to give the right nutrients to get sleepy or become active. When the food was finished and the night was over, at home the guests could still smell the light odor of the stamp that enhanced their food memory. During the performance weeks we made an information chart on the walls, by having people stick their used spoons in it after eating. This way it became public knowledge whether Amsterdam was in need of energy or relaxation.

Energy is the ability to achieve change   the physical energy of a system

- Trout is full of omega-3 acids and zinc. Which helps against fatigue
  Trout with horseradish
- The starch in pasta provides energy and Tarragon activates the brain
  Pasta salad with tarragon
- Pear contains a lot of fruit-sugars and fibre for a balanced energy level.
  cut your own cress!
  Pear salad with cress.

Energy lunch

- 'Boeren Goudse oplegkaas' (the best Gouda cheese) with tomato jam
  When columbus brought the tomato to Europe, people thought that the fruit was causing 'love-madness' anyway this 'love-apple' gives energy!
- scrambled egg with kurkuma
  Kurkuma has a fast, stimulating effect. Because of their high-protein-level, eggs give long lasting energy.
- polenta with sage
  Sage activates the brain and helps you memorize. Polenta = corn = energy
  grate your own cheese

is the total amount of power that needs to be forced to enter from the initial groundstate to the present

Project
FIBONACCI DRINKS

About
Yoghurt and orange juice mixed in proportions that were dictated by the Fibonacci sequence instead of a chef.

Year
2006

in Mathematics, the Fibonacci numbers are a sequence of numbers named after Leonardo of Pisa, known as Fibonacci. the first number is 0, the second number is 1. and each subsequent number is equal to the sum of the previous two numbers of the sequence itself.

the changing amount is only effective when it's being applied to a constant factor.

standard bun.   1   1   2   3   5   8   13   21   34   55   89   144

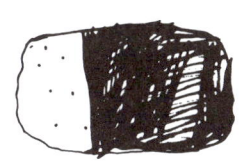

golden ratio cookie with chocolate

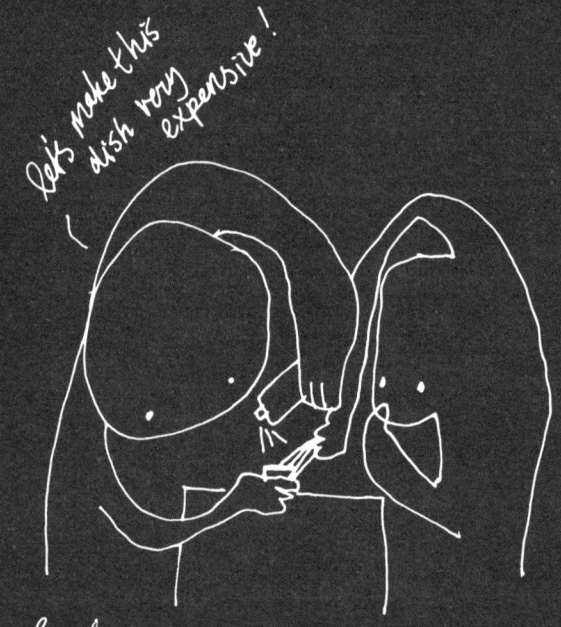

TECH NIQUE

Chapter 07

* Did you ever:
Smoke an egg?
Knit Spaghetti?
Drill holes in cheese?
Print on bread?
Dehydrate Honey?
Embroider lettuce leafs?
Bake soup?

Project
CONNECTION DINER

About
During the night before the dinner, the angle poise lamps 'cooked' the tablecloth, which was made of dough. Bowls were set up underneath the dough. Subsequently we served hot and soggy things like soup and stew that cooked the dough again and made it soft and edible. Guests all ate a part of the same 'tablecloth'. After the main course the bowls were removed to reveal a next layer of tablecloth made of pink sugar dough. On top of this we served caramelized fruits and nuts to eat with the tablecloth.

Year
2006

layer of pink sugardough

fruit and nuts

dough on top of table plus bowls and plates

decoration with herbs (gives taste too)

desk lamps are placed in various positions like a dinner-choreography choreography

Project
ARMOUR

Year
2003

breaddough:
4 parts of plain or full grain flower.
2 parts of ~~water~~ water.
one teaspoon of salt per 500 gram flower
↓ mix and knead.

use existing crockery as moulds.
take bowls, plates and cups that are heat-resistant

put them upside down and make them greasy with oil.
oil ↓

roll out the dough and put it on top of your moulds.

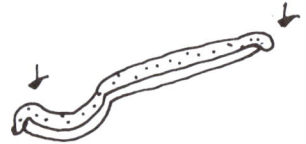

Like everyone, I was told as a child not to play with my food. (And that everything gets mixed up in your stomach anyway, so it doesn't matter what it looks like on the place. Mama, what were you thinking?!)

I think that the word playing may be confused with the idea that people should have respect for their food, and I completely agree with that. In my work, no matter how playful it may look, I always try to facilitate appreciation for food and everything around it. We have a worm composting box at Proef and we try to be responsible about purchasing and how we process waste.

Playing with food can sometimes be very useful, though. Many children brace themselves when they hear that they have to sit down to dinner. For many parents, the daily meal with their children is a cold war waged every day, armed to the teeth. It is no longer about the food, but about the power to put food in your body - or not. At a certain age, children discover that they are in control of their own body; they realise that eating broccoli or refusing to eat it is a weak point is their parents' armour. Don't mention it to people who are right in the middle of that phase... but it's actually a gorgeous choreography of action and reaction, balance and willpower, back and forth between parent and child. I know, I know, the actual practice is mainly just nerve-wracking!

But in some way I also understand quite well that it can be fairly frightening for children to try something new. Parents consider it only logical for their children to have to taste everything, but travelling to another country where the menu includes milk with clotted blood, fermented shark, living octopus or mealworms, things that you aren't used to eating, you would have to overcome your fear before you put it in your mouth.

There is something very intimate about casually putting something into your mouth and into your body. You have to have faith in the chef that prepared it. You have to know that it won't make you sick; if something really doesn't agree with you, it may make you gag. That's a very unpleasant sensation. I read a study that said that children have to taste something seven times before they will accept a new flavour. It's just like learning new words; they have to be repeated over and over.

So a child doesn't like olives the first time around? Keep trying, even if it's just one bite. The atmosphere or situation in which a food is eaten is also very important to what a child is willing to eat. My child isn't any different. Pages 60 and 61 show my lovely little Juni when she was about two and a half or three years old. Madam was a very poor vegetable eater. I thought, "That's obviously unacceptable for my profession!" Bad advertising! So I invited her and the children from her day-care centre to do a taste test. We had a table filled with vegetables, and I told them that we were going to do a jewellery-making workshop. (I called it a 'bling-bling workshop' for the rough-and-tumble boys.) The tools they were allowed to use were their teeth; anyone who's ever been bitten by one of those little darlings knows just how sharp those tiny teeth are! We also had some cut-out shapes and an electric drill, but most of it had to be done with their teeth.

The children tackled those vegetables bravely. They had to put the vegetables in their mouths to make the jewellery - but that didn't matter, because they weren't actually eating them, right? Loads of vegetables were surreptitiously nibbled up that afternoon without my young guest feeling like they had to sit down to eat. They sampled the flavours without any struggle or cold war.

I can now proudly state that Juni eats her vegetables!

Like everyone, I was told as a child not to play with my food. (And that everything gets mixed up in your stomach anyway, so it doesn't matter what it looks like on the plate. Mama, what were you thinking?!)

I think that the word playing may be confused with the idea that people should have respect for their food, and I completely agree with that. In my work, no matter how playful it may look, I always try to facilitate appreciation for food and everything around it. We have a worm composting box at Proef and we try to be responsible about purchasing and how we process waste.

Playing with food can sometimes be very useful, though. Many children brace themselves when they hear that they have to sit down to dinner. For many parents, the daily meal with their children is a cold war waged every day, armed to the teeth. It is no longer about the food, but about the power to put food in your body - or not. At a certain age, children discover that they are in control of their own body; they realise that eating broccoli or refusing to eat it is a weak point in their parents' armour. Don't mention it to people who are right in the middle of that phase… but it's actually a gorgeous choreography of action and reaction, balance and willpower, back and forth between parent and child. I know, I know, the actual practice is mainly just nerve-wracking!

But in some way I also understand quite well that it can be fairly frightening for children to try something new. Parents consider it only logical for their children to have to taste everything, but travelling to another country where the menu includes milk with clotted blood, fermented shark, living octopus or mealworms, things that you aren't used to eating, you would have to overcome your fear before you put it in your mouth.

There is something very intimate about casually putting something into your mouth and into your body. You have to have faith in the chef that prepared it. You have to know that it won't make you sick; if something really doesn't agree with you, it may make you gag. That's a very unpleasant sensation. I read a study that said that children have to taste something seven times before they will accept a new flavour. It's just like learning new words; they have to be repeated over and over.

So a child doesn't like olives the first time around? Keep trying, even if it's just one bite. The atmosphere or situation in which a food is eaten is also very important to what a child is willing to eat. My child isn't any different. Pages 60 and 61 show my lovely little Juni when she was about two and a half or three years old. Madam was a very poor vegetable eater. I thought, "That's obviously unacceptable for my profession!. Bad advertising! So I invited her and the children from her day-care centre to do a taste test. We had a table filled with vegetables, and I told them that we were going to do a jewellery-making workshop. (I called it a 'bling-bling workshop' for the rough-and-tumble boys.) The tools they were allowed to use were their teeth; anyone who's ever been bitten by one of those little darlings knows just how sharp those tiny teeth are! We also had some cut-out shapes and an electric drill, but most of it had to be done with their teeth.

The children tackled those vegetables bravely. They had to put the vegetables in their mouths to make the jewellery - but that didn't matter, because they weren't actually eating them, right? Loads of vegetables were surreptitiously nibbled up that afternoon without my young guest feeling like they had to sit down to eat. They sampled the flavours without any struggle or cold war.

I can now proudly state that Juni eats her vegetables!

also big metal spoons are useful.

Do it roughly and not too neat! the pieces should have a rough and naive look.

depending on the thickness, bake your crockery 30 minutes at 180°C
/45

Project
CRESSWEAR

garden cress
garden cress
garden cress
cress dress
(garden) cress-dress

dress to cress

grated cheese on top
← cress-sandwich

cress name or cresshair

hat

turn your child into a green monster or a hedgehog

gardencress also tastes good as a grown plant (less healthy)

this is a large piece of fabric

cocktail garnish.

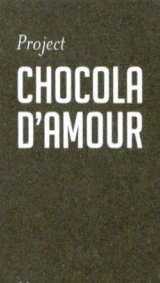

Project
CHOCOLA D'AMOUR

Year
2007

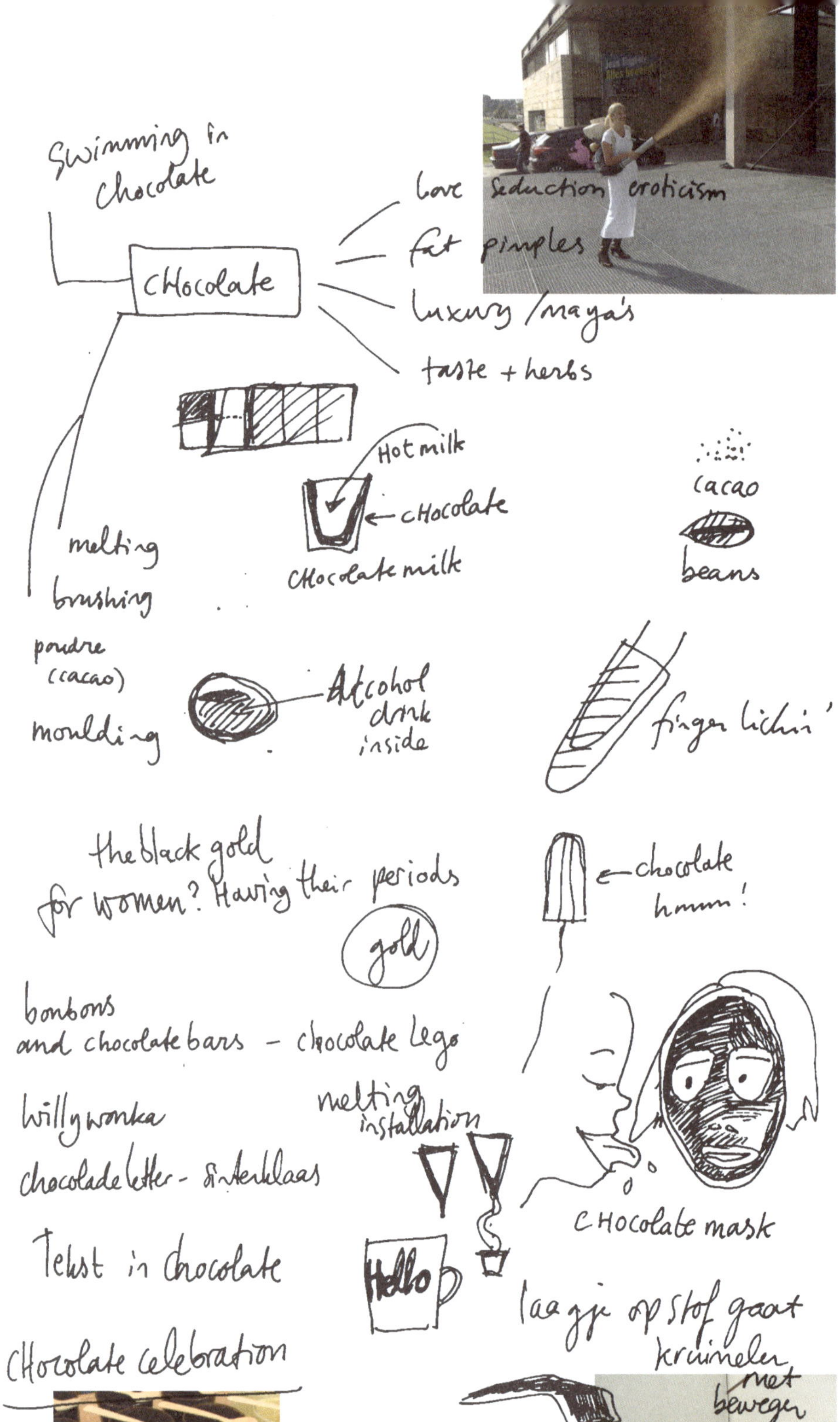

Swimming in chocolate

Chocolate
— love, seduction, eroticism
— fat, pimples
— luxury / maya's
— taste + herbs

Hot milk → chocolate
Chocolate milk

cacao beans

melting
brushing
poudre (cacao)
moulding

Alcohol drink inside

finger lickin'

the black gold for women? Having their periods — gold

← chocolate hmm!

bonbons and chocolate bars — chocolate lego

willy wonka
chocoladeletter — sinterklaas
Tekst in chocolate
Chocolate celebration

melting installation
Hello

chocolate mask

laagje op stof gaat kruimelen met bewegen

Project
MARSHMALLOW VIRUS

Year
2008

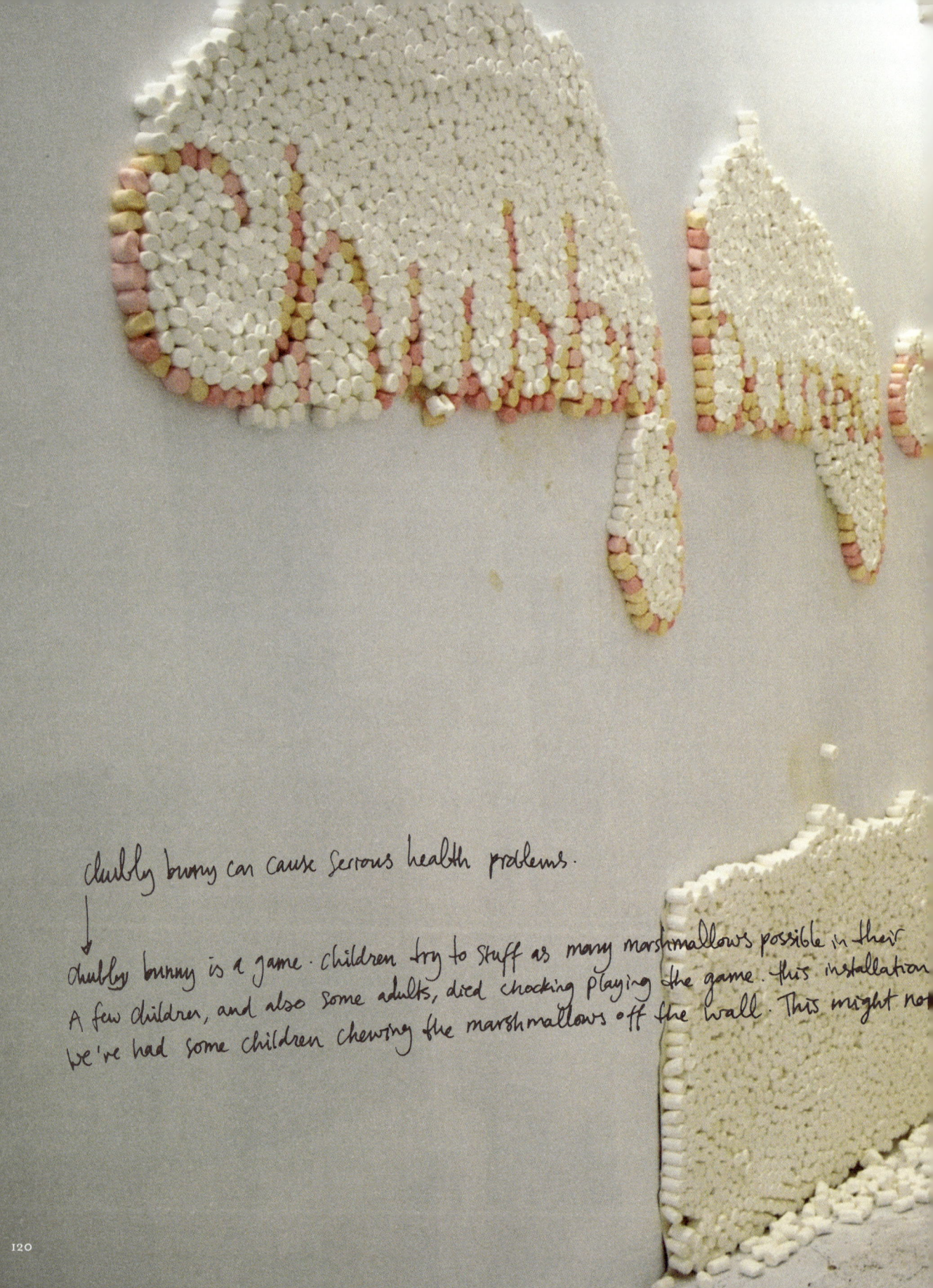

chubby bunny can cause serious health problems.

chubby bunny is a game. children try to stuff as many marshmallows possible in their
A few children, and also some adults, died chocking playing the game. this installation
we've had some children chewing the marshmallows off the wall. This might no

Cause Serious

...north. While doing this they proclaim "CHUBBY Bunny"
...has a soft touch and a sweet vanilla smell.
...cause death by 'chubby bunny' but by superglue

Project
SUGAR

I did a course in sugar-art.
Sugar pulling and blowing is an old, traditional craft.
I had to learn to make a clown, a swan and a fruit basket. Sometimes it's hard to set aside your own aesthetics in order to learn a technique.

this lollypop visualises what sugar can do to your body

If Rotterdam is the mouth of europe, then what is the arse of europe?

where do I go to?

SOCIETY

Chapter **08**

* What's wrong with mass production?
What's right with mass production?
How many fish are left in the sea?
When do we have to start eating insects for our protein needs?
To what extend do charity organisations have to deal with corruption?
Why are the poorest people eating the crappiest food?
Why is sustainable not always sustainable?
Why do we all think we need added vitamins?
How far does my pineapple travel?
How often do you eat alone?
What does E124 mean?

"You might just as well invent new animals"

Rice has been for centuries the most important component of Indonesian cooking. Under the influence of Dutch colonisation (late 16th until mid 20th century), however, unpolished rice fell out of favour. Even though this rice contained healthy bran and fibre, the Dutch refined it by removing the germ and outer layers, leaving a white grain which would henceforth count as a sign of prosperity and civilisation. That this 'improvement' meant that a large part of the nutritional value was lost was not a problem for the colonists and wealthy citizens. After all, they could always get their necessary nutrients from vegetables, fish and meat. But for the poor, who continue to eat almost nothing but rice, it meant an impoverishment of their diet with all the health problems that this entails.

A natural propensity for healthy food and good crops was not only impaired in Indonesia. It seems a long time ago that the climate and the changes of the seasons determined how crops and species of animals would thrive somewhere, thus also harmonising with food and eating rituals in different parts of the world. Yet the expression 'from time immemorial' no longer has the implications in the year 2008 that it always had. As a result of the explosive growth of transport and new, super-fast methods of cultivation, strawberries and runner beans can be eaten all year round in Northern Europe where they are only harvested during a single season. When the temperature falls in the North they are simply flown in from Southern Spain or Egypt. What's more, not only the ingredients but virtually all dishes are available everywhere in the world. This is due not only to cooks fanning out worldwide from all continents, but also to the drastic standardisation of our food, a 'McDonaldization' that has slowly but surely alienated us from our original way of dealing with food. Everywhere in the world we can buy exactly the same food in the same supermarkets.[7] Not only has this removed part of the surprise of foreign travel but it has also meant a loss of all sorts of traditional methods of production, less diversity of crops and a decrease in the types of food available. In the year 2008 it is becoming increasingly clear that these developments are even disastrous for the environment (the burning of fossil fuels needed for production, packaging and transport releases huge amounts of greenhouse gases into the atmosphere) and have led to numerous so-called diseases of civilisation, including obesity (see note 5).

OK, I've said it before. I'm not a food designer; food is already perfectly designed by nature. There are more aspects that I don't do than things that I am doing. I'm not a chef, a farmer, a nutritionist or a food technologist. Designers can't do all of anything and can do a little of everything. But the nice thing about this position, the position of a creative thinker, is that I have the chance to move between all sorts of different professions, working across the boundaries of specialisations. In my profession, I can bring the food technologist into contact with the farmer, link them to the mother feeding her child, the politician contemplating the Commodities Act, the marketer, the cook, the consumer and the behavioural scientist. I am not a specialist; I'm a first aid kit, patching people up. I bind various professions together and hope they knit together. Cross-pollinate each other, or possibly eat each other whole?

Sure, of course it's fun to make a wedding cake. The happy couple will be ecstatic with the result, but the project is not challenging as such. Can a creative person do something to counteract the collapse of bee colonies? Or exploitation? Can we come up with something to solve the waste problem, social isolation, or obesity?

I think you can. I think that everyone can do something about problems like that based on their own capabilities. And I think that people who work as creative professionals and also use their creativity to help brainstorm solutions for the most urgent issues. Maybe the solution will not be a physical object, but it also has to be possible to think in terms of intangible solutions.

That's why I want to call on all creative thinkers to focus that creativity on the more difficult things in the world. We may not be able to save the world, but I do think that we can create more awareness and inspire people to do things differently. We can't just leave it all up to politicians and activists. Free thinkers can build bridges - and the world still needs a lot of patching up!

OK, I've said it before. I'm not a food designer; food is already perfectly designed by nature. There are more aspects that I don't do than things that I am doing. I'm not a chef, a farmer, a nutritionist or a food technologist. Designers can't do all of anything and can do a little of everything. But the nice thing about this position, the position of a creative thinker, is that I have the chance to move between all sorts of different professions, working across the boundaries of specialisations. In my profession, I can bring the food technologist into contact with the farmer, link them to the mother feeding her child, the politician contemplating the Commodities Act, the marketer, the cook, the consumer and the behavioural scientist. I am not a specialist; I'm a first aid kit, patching people up. I bind various professions together and hope they knit together. Cross-pollinate each other, or possibly eat each other whole?

Sure, of course it's fun to make a wedding cake. The happy couple will be ecstatic with the result, but the project is not challenging as such. Can a creative person do something to counteract the collapse of bee colonies? Or exploitation? Can we come up with something to solve the waste problem, social isolation, or obesity?

I think you can. I think that everyone can do something about problems like that based on their own capabilities. And I think that people who work as creative professionals and also use their creativity to help brainstorm solutions for the most urgent issues. Maybe the solution will not be a physical object, but it also has to be possible to think in terms of intangible solutions.

That's why I want to call on all creative thinkers to focus that creativity on the more difficult things in the world. We may not be able to save the world, but I do think that we can create more awareness and inspire people to do things differently. We can't just leave it all up to politicians and activists. Free thinkers can build bridges - and the world still needs a lot of patching up!

Last but certainly not least, rapid production methods are at the expense of the value we attach to experiencing food. 1986 saw the opening of the umpteenth McDonald's restaurant in Rome and, as a protest, the Slow Food movement was born in Italy. The movement, an affiliation of mainly small-scale businesses, propagates natural ingredients, local products and slow, traditional methods of preparation.[8]

That Marije Vogelzang often works with Slow Food products is a logical choice. "But I don't regard natural ingredients and the preparing of healthy food as an aim in itself. What matters to me is the experience of eating in this specific company and in this specific context at this moment. The whole story. I have a mission - it sounds terrible, but that's what it is. I'm convinced that it contributes to a feeling of happiness when people know where the things they eat come from, how they are prepared and what meanings and stories are attached to them. That's why it is logical that I use ingredients that are locally cultivated, belong to the season in which they are eaten and are prepared according to traditional methods that do justice to the taste and experience. This means that in the Netherlands I prefer to work with hazelnuts, savory, nettles or sorrel and only sparingly with basil, for example, that is more suited to the weather conditions in Italy. Yet I'm not a blind adept of Slow Food. Since I'm primarily interested in the experiential quality I'm not a supporter of a specific type of cooking for reasons of health, ideology or morals. I'm not a purist, not a vegetarian, not a vegan, nor a macrobiotic or raw foodist, and I don't want to work just with organically grown products.[9] Sometimes industrially prepared dishes are more suited to a project. And if the event or the assignment calls for it I also work with elements like food dyes and sugar which are not per se 'healthy'. But I must admit that these are exceptions."

Project
FAKED MEAT

Year
2008

That she does not allow herself to be easily pinned down to a particular type of cooking or tradition and has a lighthearted approach to the theme of 'good food' is evident from *Faked Meat*, a project that is still very much in the process of being developed. Faked Meat started as a reaction to the meat substitutes that supermarkets have had on their shelves for a long time already, sometimes even amidst the 'real' meat products. Tofu, for example, can be made in the form of cutlets that, with the addition of spices, are hardly distinguishable from the meat versions. Even in health shops we find mixtures of protein and vegetables marketed as sausages. "You might just as well invent new animals. Why not play God?", thought Vogelzang and then started fantasising about the possibilities of bringing food design and animal design close together. "Food Designer Katja Gruijters was studying in the same department as I and in 1998 she had made a series of forms in response to meat substitutes, which didn't look like meat at all.

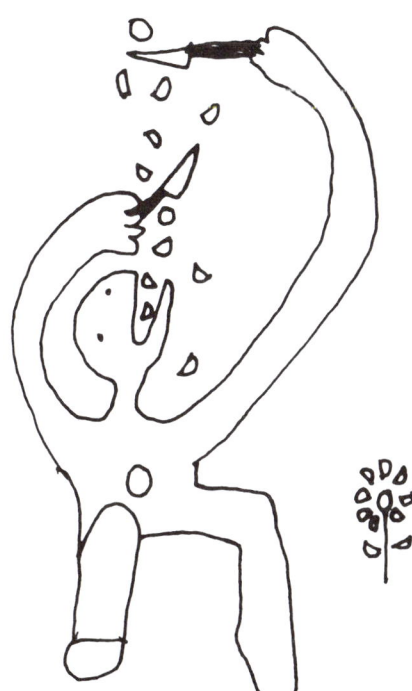

A very successful project, but as far as I know it was never actually produced. For one reason or another we are so programmed that we associate animals with nice food. So with my designs I wanted to refer to animals but then to animals that don't yet exist." To each new species of animal Vogelzang couples a story about its way of life and natural habitat. One of them, for example, lives in volcanoes and this gives a slightly smoked taste to its flesh, while its long, stiff tail makes it highly suitable as a party snack. Another animal is square shaped so that a cook can easily cut slices. A fish with decorative green stripes, by which the connoisseur can see that it contains a high proportion of anti-oxidants, can easily be transformed into sushi - these divine creatures make a lighthearted nod to the rationalised world of efficient food production.

Herbast - *Detragono Erbalis*

The Herbast originates from Greece and southern Albania, they feast on a rich diet of aromatic plants, resulting in their flavoured fat and a herb fur-coat. This works not only as a camouflage but also gives Herbast it's distinctive herbal taste.

With their natural seasoning and convenient square shape, Herbast is the perfect "ready-to-use" meat, ideal for many dishes from different BBQ cuts to Sunday roasts and carpaccios.

Herbast-stir fry   *Serves 2, main course*

1 package (200 g) herbast-cubes
1 medium sized onion, finely chopped
1 red pepper, coarsely chopped
6 medium sized tomatoes, coarsely chopped
Olive oil
Salt
Black pepper

Heat a frying pan with olive oil and fry the onion until slightly soft, about a minute. Add the Herbast-cubes and continue frying, until nicely coloured. The herbs will now separate from the meat and a wonderful rich scent will develop. Add the chopped pepper and tomatoes, simmer slowly for 15 minutes, allowing the flavours to increase their intensity.
Serve with couscous, rice or your own choice of carbohydrates.

Whole roasted Herbast   *Serves 8, as a main course*

1,5 kg herbast-roast
Olive oil
Salt
Black pepper

Preheat the oven to 175 °C.
Add salt and pepper to the four sides. Put in an ovenproof dish, slightly buttered, and place in the oven. Use a cooking thermometer and cook until the inner temperature reaches 60°C, for juicy medium rare, or 70 °C for well done. Rest for 15 minutes, slice and serve.

Tip: Enjoy Herbast-roast with baked vegetables and fresh goat's cheese.

Sapicu – *Avicularis Atrovirens*

The Sapicu lives in the Canadian maple trees where it gets all its nutrients from the sap and leaves. The Sapicu's picky diet makes them an exquisite treat to savour. The sugary sap works as a marinade tenderising the Sapicu, developing its juicy and sweet flavour, that is best compared to the flesh of a lychee fruit.
Sapicu is a perfect dessert to finish off a summer meal, slowly cooked with a caramelized crust served together with a creamy vanilla ice cream.

Caramelized Sapicu *Serves 2, as a desert*

2 Sapicu fillets
Vanilla ice cream

Preheat the oven grill.
Put the two Sapicu fillets in an ovenproof dish and place in the oven. Cook until the surface is caramelized with a nice golden colour. Serve with vanilla ice cream.

Sapicu-wings with dark chocolate
Serves 2, dessert

1 package of Sapicu wings
100 g 70 % dark chocolate
1 dl cream
1 egg yolk, optional

Chop the chocolate finely. Bring the cream to the boil and pour over the chocolate. Stir until completely melted. For a richer and creamier sauce, fold in the yolk and stir gently until smooth. Pour the chocolate over the two wings, let cool and serve.

Project
CUDDLY SAUSAGE

About
I live in the city. When I look around I hardly see any animals. I might see some pets but rarely I see the animals that I eat and I never see them being slaughtered. When my daughter looks around she sees mostly cuddly animals. When she watches TV she sees them in cartoons wearing clothes and doing a little dance. At the kids farm around the corner the animals are considered cute and her animal toys all have big eyes and pink furs. This 200 kg cuddly sausage was mostly made of meat from animals that have large natural living spaces. By pulling the string, the knitting would unravel and reveal the elegantly flavoured sausage inside.

Year
2008

The binding strength of food

"Marije uses food as material, no more and no less", says Li Edelkoort, the trend forecaster and Vogelzang's former teacher. "The main thing she has added to the field is a consciousness of the ritual aspect of eating, the emotion. By nature she has a sort of rural simplicity. But then a simplicity that transcends itself. I saw her enter the academy as a teenager who had grown up too fast, clumsy in her movements, but with an incredible dedication and passion. She definitely had it in in her to become an international star in her profession. You could best describe her as a dish with precisely the right ingredients: a non-conventional originality and great personal charm, authenticity, courage, humour, and a view on her field and on her own role in it. She has taste, a good feeling for aesthetics and the visual strength of an artist. And what's also very important, she has the gift of being able to renew herself each time. She is a work in progress." Similar words also come from the designer Hella Jongerius in whose office Vogelzang worked for a year as a junior designer. She particularly praises her former employee's enterprise. "Many young designers behave like spoilt children who wait for the most ideal assignment before they start undertaking something. Marije dares to take risks, she sticks her neck out. She's sure to go far in the world."

Project
**KHOBZ W MELH
ON THE GREEN LINE**

Year
2008

Taste of Beirut
workshop by Marije Vogelzang and Souk el Tayeb

All the ingredients to become an international star. Yet if you talk with Marije Vogelzang you'll soon notice that fame is not her primary motive. "It's just something that I really like doing." Perhaps the secret of her success lies in the passion with which she examines each assignment for its potential. Over the course of time she has unmistakably developed a visual signature of her own. But as soon as a project calls for a design in which Vogelzang is less recognisably present, then there's not a moment's hesitation in going for the content. With a project in Beirut it quickly became clear that it "should not be about this Dutch designer. The most important thing was the experience of the participants and so they also had to be able to determine the design. I am an aesthete and usually retain control over the design, but here it would have been absurd if I had stuck to my own aesthetic preferences."

In the spring of 2008 Vogelzang came in contact with Kamal Mouzawak, a Lebanese chef, TV personality and writer who had created the first farmers market in Beirut in 2004.[10] "In Lebanon we have many different religious sects with seemingly nothing in common", Mouzawak said. "Except food. Muslims and Christians in the north eat the same food. Muslims and Christians in the south eat the same food. The differences are regional."[11] Lebanon was divided by sectarian and political conflicts but the market, Souk el Tayeb (tasty market) soon grew into a symbol of national unity.[12]

And don't forget:
The joy of eating!

And don't forget:
The joy of eating!

Souk el tayeb every Saturday in Saifi Village parking, Beirut every Sunday in Zouk Mikael, upper souk, Beirut.

Recognizing in Vogelzang a like-minded spirit, Mouzawak invited her to come to Lebanon to work on the *Taste of Beirut* project. Although only her travel costs would be paid, Vogelzang was so enthusiastic and attracted by the subject that she devised a workshop and presentation called *Khobz w Melh on the Green Line* (meaning literally 'like salt and bread on the Green Line'; when you have a good bond with one another then you are inextricably bound together 'like salt and bread'). "First of all I immersed myself in the history of the city and Arab cooking. Then I asked the participants in the workshop, people from various backgrounds, of different ages, religious movements and political views, to answer a list of questions about their memories of food. Many of the answers confirmed what I already know from other experiences: people everywhere in the world mainly have fond memories of the food that their mother or grandmother used to cook for them. I decided to make basins of bread with the participants because almost everyone has written that they associated bread with both peacetime and war. What's more, bread is a great metaphor. As people we are essentially alike, made of the same dough, but we all have a different, unique form. So the bowls would also assume different forms, kneaded by individuals from a range of backgrounds. The dough was coloured green by mixing it with parsley juice, the most important herb in Lebanese cooking. After the forms were baked the participants wrote their favourite stories onto them with sugar. Then the green bowls were filled with typical Lebanese food and presented on a long line of tables running right through the market. The people ate both the contents and the bowls themselves, thereby digesting other people's memories as it were." The colour of Khobz w Melh on the Green Line referred to the division of Beirut. During the Lebanese civil war (1975-1990) the so-called Green Line separated West Beirut, mostly home to Muslims, from East Beirut, the domain of the Christian sections of the population. Since the strip was uninhabited, overgrown vegetation gave the division the appearance of a green line. "I wanted to symbolically change that fact into something positive. We eat not only to feed our body, but also our mind. And what is perhaps the most important thing: eating brings people together."

Project
EVERYBODY IS AN EGG

About
Presenting food in a vertical position instead of horizontally makes you think of picking food from a tree or bush. 'Everybody is an egg' was a range of snacks that were all made of eggs, prepared differently. Boiling, frying, poaching, fluffy egg white, mayonnaise… eggs have so many appearances. The project referred to us humans. We all have a very different appearance but we are all made from the same ingredients.

Year
2005

Project
SUSTAINABILITY DINNER

About
Does food that has come from afar taste better? In this project the starters communicated the distance and origin of the ham and melon classic... Finding the specific food was our chef's nightmare by the way. Food prepared in the old, energy saving way in hay-boxes. The food waited underneath the tablecloth for a few starter courses to be cooked in the meantime and ready to be discovered and tasted.

Year
2007

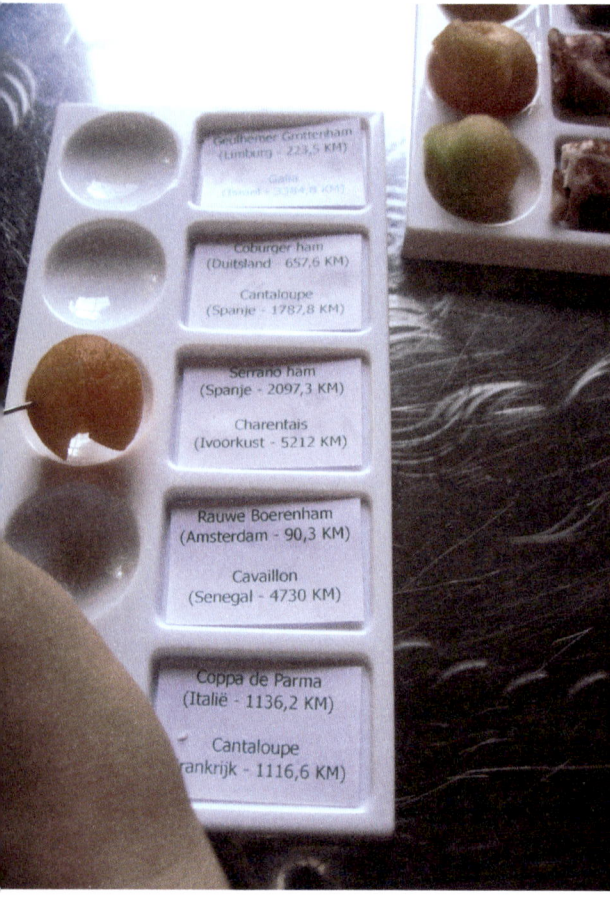

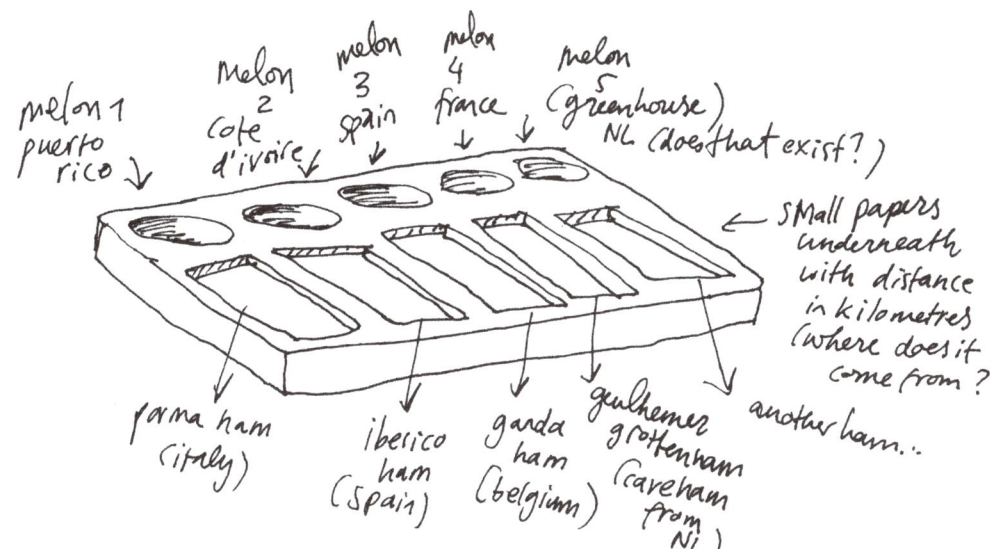

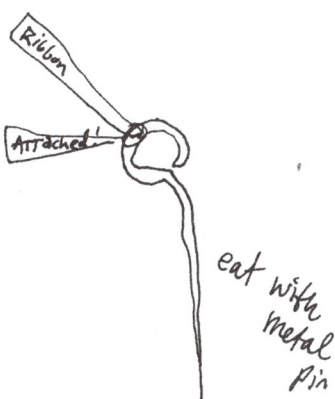

Project
PASTA SAUNA

About
Pasta Sauna was a performance I did last year in New York based on Marinetti's futurist cookbook (1920) and by courtesy of Performa 09. We made a 'pasta sauna' out of a greenhouse sauna and linked the pasta machines, which were placed on ladders, to musical boxes. By turning the handle, the pasta machines simultaneously made music and pasta. As the long sheets of pasta were made by the performers, you could hear different tunes. The space was filled with steam from the boiling water, creating a sauna. The super fresh (and very tasty!) pasta was served simply with oil, pepper, salt, fresh herbs, lemon juice and Parmesan cheese.

Year
2009

Project
GO SLOW

About
Although I only did the food for this Droog project, it was a great experience working with elderly people, creating a slow experience in the busy Milan design week. With 5 elderly couples, flown in from Eindhoven, we created simple food by hand. The oranges were pressed by hand, the cream was whipped by hand, the nuts were cracked by hand etc. Our goal was to focus all our attention to the food, transferring that focus via the food and our hospitality to the visitor, who would actually eat our focused attention. It was later performed again in Tokyo, and again in 2009 at Pioneers of Change, a festival of Dutch design, fashion and architecture on Governors Island in NYC. It was a part of the NY400 celebrations, commemorating the 400th anniversary of the arrival of the Dutch in New York. Over 25,000 visitors took the ferry.

Year
2004

Project

MOUTH WATERING SPOONS

Year
2010

About

In 2010 Droog purchased 5135 items saved from liquidation sales and other leftovers. When Renny Ramakers of Droog asked me to do something with one of these items, I immediately chose the spoons. Although, I have to say, I was tempted by the dog baskets. Initially I thought designing something with these spoons would be a piece of cake; for some reason, though, it wasn't easy. First of all, these spoons were a kind of b-choice lot. Varying in shape, size and wood. Eventually I covered the spoon with different layers of silicone in various textures. This makes it seem as if the spoons are covered with cake batter. I like the way that silicone offers possibilities for creating a very textured surface and playing with this idea. It gives the spoons a less slick appearance. Food itself is seldom slick.

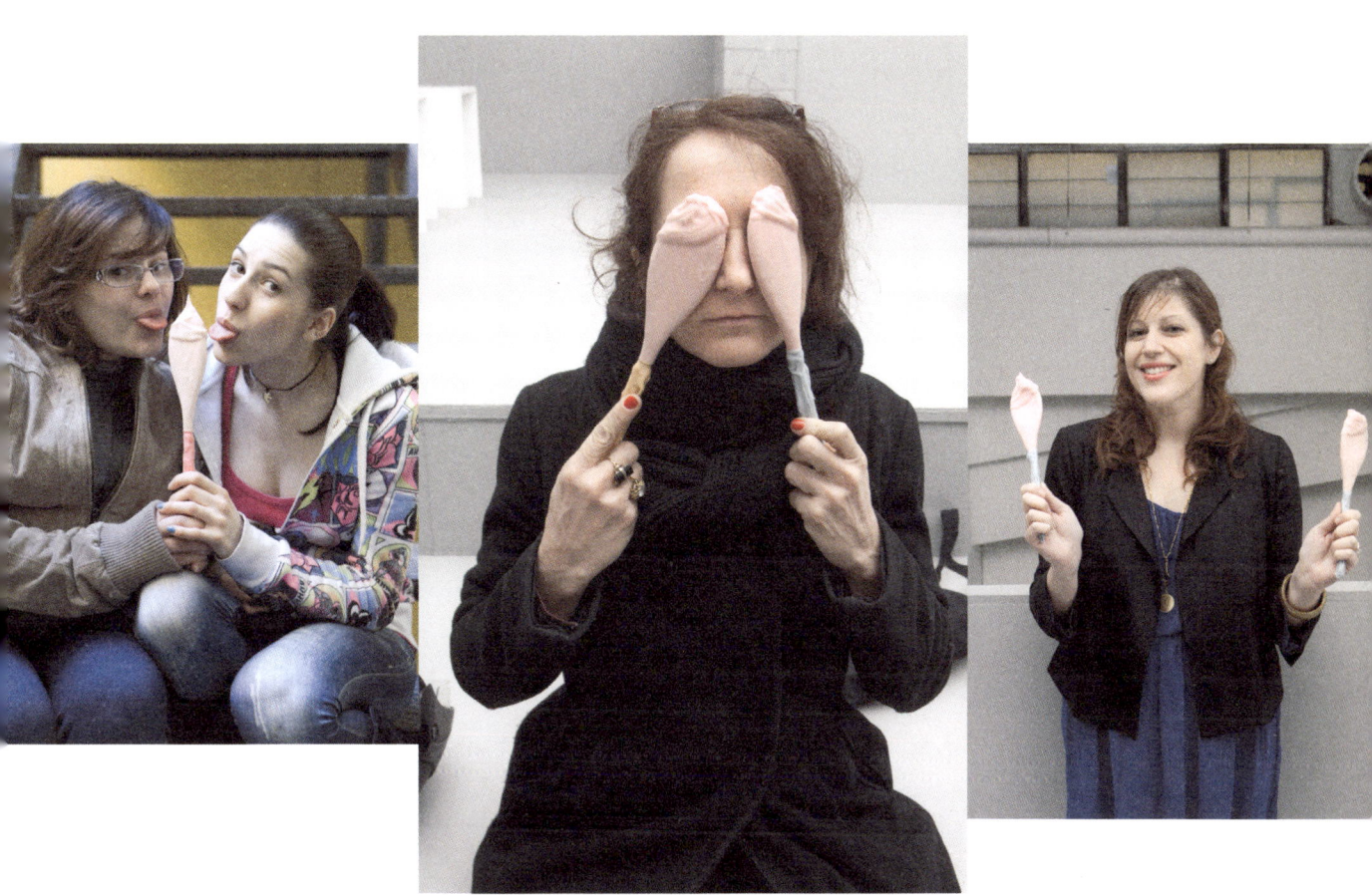

Project
BLIND DATE

About
Blind Date is a project I did with the students in the Master of Design Studies programme at Virginia Commonwealth University in Doha, Qatar. It was a three-day project trying to make an eating design project about the Islamic culture, combining patterns, textures, colours and taste with the double meaning of the words BLIND DATE.

Blind Date is a date-tasting event, but it also refers to the Islamic culture where dating is not allowed and marriages are frequently arranged. We tenderly fed various dates to the blindfolded participants and asked them to describe the taste experience. Eventually the tasters picked their 'perfect date'. At that point, we told them the country that their perfect date came from and gave them the seeds in a small envelope for them to plant back home, so they could grow their perfect date themselves.

Year
2010

Notes

1. 'Second World War' refers to a number of wars that took place in various parts of the world between 1939 and 1945. The aggressors were Germany, Italy and Japan.
For the Netherlands the war began with the German invasion on 10 May 1940. On 14 May at around 13.30 p.m. Rotterdam was bombed in order to force the country to capitulate. Within fifteen minutes more than 24,000 houses and other buildings were razed to the ground and more than 800 inhabitants killed. After the war a sculpture by Ossip Zadkine was erected in the rebuilt centre of Rotterdam. As a metaphor for the devastated city, the sculpture had the form of a human figure with a cavity for a heart. After all, the city had suffered a wound that would remain deeply etched in the memory of the inhabitants of Rotterdam. A few years after the bombardment, during the so-called *'hunger winter'* of 1944-1945, food supplies in Rotterdam had sunk to an all time low. On 6 May 1945 the Netherlands was liberated by the Americans and the war ended.

2. During the War of the Bavarian Succession (1778-79), Prussia and Austria tried to cut off food supplies to each other's army. Since there were hardly any hostilities the conflict was nicknamed the *'potato war'* (sources include http://www.encyclopedia.com).
In 2006 a satirical article in the German newspaper Die Tageszeitung led to a small but vehement *'Kartoffelkrieg'* between Poland and Germany. The newspaper called the Polish president Lech Kaczynski and his twin brother Jaroslaw, the prime minister, new potatoes, thus stirring up an old controversy between the two countries (sources include http://www.spiegel.de).
And then there was the Potato War between Peru and Chile. The United Nations declared 2008 to be the Year of the Potato, so as to promote the role of the potato in solving the worldwide food crisis. There immediately arose a difference of opinion about the origin of the plant, with politicians and scientists from Peru and Chile both disputing the birthright. For the time being the Potato War remains undecided. What is certainly clear is that the potato has a very long history that, according to most historians, starts with the Incas. The plant was 'discovered' by the Spanish when they murderously conquered and plundered what is now Chile and Peru around 1536. Chronicles of that period describe the potato as a plant with mealy roots and tasting good. In the Netherlands it was cultivated as a curiosity in botanical gardens until, starting in the 18th century, it became a familiar and popular food, which it continues to be to this day. Many a Dutchman, on being asked, will suggest that the potato is a typical Dutch product… perhaps a good reason for a new potato war (source: http://geschiedenis.vpro.nl/artikelen/39704967).

3. Since the late Eighties, Dutch designers have been making semi-functional, conceptual products that particularly stimulate the imagination. Several of them have made presentations under the flag of *Droog*, which was set up in 1993 as a platform for conceptual design. Despite their diversity, what unites these designers as a group is the way they work on the basis of their own fascinations and ideas and an aesthetic that matches these ideas. The first generation produced products that, directly or indirectly, commented on their own field, while the later generations mainly focus on the narrative quality of their work. Well-known conceptual product designers from the beginning are Jurgen Bey, Tejo Remy, Hella Jongerius, Richard Hutten and Piet Hein Eek. Among the later generation are Job Smeets, Wieki Somers, Marije Vogelzang, Bertjan Pot and Maarten Baas.

4. Marije Vogelzang is Dutch and, remarkably enough, in her native country mourning is linked to the colour black. There are virtually no food-related rituals connected with mourning in the Netherlands; after a funeral one is simply offered a cup of coffee with a slice of cake of generally dubious quality.

5. Dangerous overweight, or obesity, is usually established according to the Body Mass Index: BMI, which is based on the ratio of weight to height. The BMI can be calculated by dividing a person's body weight by the square of their height. Overweight adults have a BMI over 25, while a number above 30 indicates that they are obese. *"Overweight and obesity has reached epidemic proportions in the United States, as well as worldwide. Data collected by the National Center for Health Statistics indicate that the prevalence of obesity has increased from 12.8% in 1976-1980 to 22.5% in 1988-1994 and 30% in 1999-2000. Roughly 31% of American adults meet the criterion for obesity – about 59 million American adults. More than 64% of the US adult population have a BMI>=25 kg/m."*
(source: http://www.obesity.org)
Health problems like obesity and diabetes are largely attributed to the consumption of industrially prepared fast food. Scientific research shows that the quality of many snacks is so poor that overweight American children are as malnourished as African children who weigh precisely too little. Serious health problems thus arise, paradoxically enough, both through a lack of foodstuffs as through excesses of (unhealthy) foodstuffs. *"The hungry and the overweight share high levels of sickness and disability, shortened life expectancies, and lower levels of productivity. (…) The century with the greatest potential to eliminate malnutrition instead saw it boosted to record levels,"* says Gary Gardner, co-author with Brian Halweil of *Underfed and Overfed: The Global Epidemic of Malnutrition.* Worldwatch Paper #150, 2000.

6. The reproduction of design and architecture in the media has gained more and more importance during the last half-century. As a result, the iconographic power of objects and buildings often overshadows their actual use-value. The picture of a notable chair in a design magazine endows the design with its image and value, supplanting the thing itself, as it were. However, an experience, particularly one of eating, which is what Vogelzang is aiming at in her projects, cannot be replaced by a photograph. Yet, as is evident from the hundreds of photographs that in the meantime exist of her projects, the experience is part of her design and hence visible in the photographs.

7. The American sociologist George Ritzer used McDonald's in 2000 as a metaphor for the global consumption society that requires food to be produced, transported and consumed as quickly, efficiently and cheaply as possible. This has resulted in worldwide food production being rationalised with the aid of technology, standardization of the products on offer and homogenisation of shopping formulas. Ritzer, G. (2000), *The McDonaldization thesis. Explorations and extensions.* London, Sage. Quoted in Dagevos, H., *Voedsel als uitdrukking van een levenswijze? Een sociologische benadering.* Ethische Perspektieven 14 (2004).

8. Because of the ideological and culinary aims, as well as the relatively high costs attendant on slow methods of production, Slow Food has until now mainly been popular amongst the cultural upper classes. At a lower level the influence is noticeable in that supermarkets, for example, are offering increasing variety in the types of food on offer. Relatively expensive organic products are on the same shelves as cheap mass products. The choice is left to the customer.

9. *Vegetarians* eat no meat, fish, crustaceans or poultry. There are various degrees of vegetarianism. *Lactovegetarians* abstain from eating eggs and cheese, but do eat milk and dairy products. Stricter vegetarians, or *Vegans*, also eat no dairy products or honey, for example, because they reject any exploitation of animals. *Fruitarians* only eat raw or dried fruits, nuts, seeds, vegetable oils and sometimes honey. Vegetarianism is not restricted just to food, but also has consequences in other areas. The vegetarian will wear no fur nor, if possible, leather and use no medicines, cosmetics and other products obtained from animals. A recent trend in the vegetarian philosophy, popular among many Hollywood stars, is Raw Food cuisine, where the daily food consists of organically farmed vegetables, fruit, seaweed, nuts, wild plants, sprouted whole grains, beans and seeds. Baking, frying and boiling are absolutely forbidden in Raw Food cuisine. Grinding is allowed, as is heating, but only between 38° and 45°. *Macrobiotics* is an Eastern philosophy of life in which food occupies a central position. The macrobiotic assumes that people are healthy and happy when they live in accordance with the laws of nature. This means that the opposing forces of 'Yin' and 'Yang', terms that within the dietetics are ascribed to certain ingredients and combinations of ingredients, always have to be in balance in order to prevent diseases like cancer.
Biodynamic farms comply with the EU legislation on biodynamic agriculture. This means that no artificial compost and chemical pesticides are used, but only natural pest and weed controls and fertilizers, such as liquid manure and compost. The soil is kept fertile by rotating crops. For livestock breeding in this sector there are standards applying to accommodation, feeds and concentrates, permitted medicines (no antibiotics or growth hormones) and norms relating to the breeding of new animals (sources include: http://www.vegetariers.nl, http://michmyer1.tripod.com/Voeding.htm, http://www.veganisme.org, http://www.elsevier.nl, http://www.nvvm.org, http://www.runnersweb.nl).

10. The contact was established through culinary journalists Merijn Tol and Nadia Zerouali, who were working at the time on a book about the differences and similarities in Arab Mediterranean culinary traditions.

11. Anna Sussman, *A Lebanese chef's vision: Make falafel, not war.* The International Herald Tribune, August 16, 2007.

12. Souk = gathering place / market. Tayeb = good, related to *taste*, to the *character* of a person, but also to something or somebody being *alive*. Good taste, good energy and life are the ingredients of *Souk el Tayeb* (for more information see www.soukeltayeb.com).

Curriculum Vitae (short version)

I only eat canned food

2011
- Malnutrition program development for Groene Hart hospital, Gouda, NL.
- Consultancy: Xue Xue institute, Taipei, Taiwan
- Consultancy: Blooming Hotel, Bergen, NL
- Consultancy: healthy snacks for Albert Heijn, NL
- Lecture at *Orebro University*, Grythytten Academy, *School of Hospitality, Culinary Arts & Meal Science*, Sweden
- Lecture at Agro Food Park, Arhus, Denmark
- *White Lunch* Bugaboo international press presentation. Amsterdam, NL.
- *Flock of Cheese* pop-up shop Everyday Dutch featuring Dutch Design at Selfridges. London, UK.

2010
Lectures
- Lecture at CreaPro, Kiev, Ukraine.
- Lecture at Head Space Symposium. Parsons The New School for Design and The Museum of Modern Art (MoMA), in partnership with International Flavors & Fragrances Inc. (IFF), Coty Inc. and Seed. New York, USA.
- Lecture at European Food Service Summit. Stockholm, Sweden.
- Lecture at TEDx Munich. Munich, Germany.
- Lecture at University of Michigan School of Art & Design's Penny W. Stamps Distinguished Speaker Series. Detroit, Michigan.
- Lecture at Gain: Design (Re)Invents AIGA Design and Business Conference. New York, USA.

Projects
- Kids concept for *Nandos restaurants, London, UK*
- *Concultancy for Future laboratory, (absolute) London, UK*
- *Inspiration session for WGSN, the leading online trend-analysis and research center, London, UK*
- *Mouth Watering Spoons*, wooden spoons dipped in silicone for *Saved by Droog*. Milan, Italy.
- Wall decorations for the restaurants of the Dutch Parliament building, The Hague, NL.
- Workshop: *Blind Date*, blind-date tasting workshop with the masters programme of Virginia Commonwealth University around eating design in Islamic culture. Doha, Quatar.
- Interactive dinner *Bits and Bytes*, for the opening exhibition by Atelier van Lieshout at the Submarine Wharf for Museum Boijmans van Beuningen and the Rotterdam Port Authority. Rotterdam, NL.
- For Louis Vuitton *Best of Amsterdam*, snacks made from the best ingredients and producers of their Amsterdam Opening Bijenkorf Shop and Opening Exhibition at the Rijksmuseum. Amsterdam, NL.
- Workshops: *Milk Bar*, blind milk tasting and cheesemaking for children in Theater aan het Spui. The Hague, NL.
- *Energy Dinner* for Ciudad de las Ideas. Puebla, Mexico.
- *Mendini flight of butterflies bites* for the re-opening of the Groninger Museum. Groningen, NL.
- Exhibition *Bread Mom*, a mother figure made of bread for the Tutti a Tavola! Exhibition in Galleria d'Arte Moderna. Milan, Italy.

- Brainstorm for Schiphol
- Brainstorm for Osage
- Brainstorm for Hak
- Brainstorm for Studio Room

Catering and groups at Proef Restaurant:
IDTV, Volvo, Ahold, Ymere, Kunstenaars&Co, Happinez, Eigen Huis & Tuin, Gemeente Den Haag, Nespresso, GE, Levi's, Buitenlandse Zaken, Mojo, Dutch DFA, Elsevier, KRO. IKEA, NIPO, Adidas, Louis Vuitton Christmas event Bijenkorf en PC Hooftstraat and many others.

2009
Books
- Publication of *EAT LOVE*, BIS Publishers.
- Publication of *Broodtrommelboek*, Uitgeverij SNOR.

Lectures
- Lecture at Food & Design Conference. Stavanger, Norway.
- Lecture at Design Blast Conference. Karlsruhe, Germany.
- Lecture at LYNfabrikken. Arhus&Kopenhagen. Denmark.
- Lecture at Festival of European Culture. Strasbourgh, France.
- Lecture at HAS Food Design & Innovation. Den Bosch, NL.
- Lecture at 10th European Foodservice Summit, Setting a Course for a New Horizon. Zurich, Germany.
- Lecture at Puratos, Center for Bread Flavour. Ardennes, Belgium.
- Lecture at Pop! Tech. New York, USA.
- Lecture and *EAT LOVE* dinner at Ciudad de las Ideas. Puebla, Mexico.
- Lecture at Design Conference for The Israel Museum. Jerusalem, Israel.
- Lecture at Tallinn Applied Art Triennale, Estonian Museum of Applied Art and Design, Tallinn, Estonia.

Projects
- Fruit and vegetables design for Groente en Fruitburo. Honselersdijk, NL.
- *Sustainable Stew*, a seminar and dinner for DDC-I (Dutch Design Center) on Design in Change. Utrecht, NL.
- *Colour food*, a food installation based on colour for Dutch DFA at DMY International Design Festival. Berlin, Germany.
- *Roots and Sharing*, dinner for the board of KPN at the Rijksakademie. Amsterdam, NL.
- *Go Slow Cafe*, Pioneers of Change, on New York's Governors Island as part of the NY400 celebrations, commemorating the 400th anniversary of the arrival of the Dutch to New York. Commissioned by Droog Design. New York, USA.
- *Urban Architecture*, dinner for ARCAM, Amsterdam Centre for Architecture. Amsterdam, NL.
- *Weather Dinner*, dinner with weather elements for UPC. Amsterdam, NL.
- *Baby Shower Bread*, for Quooker tap 'Twins' at the Woonbeurs. Amsterdam, NL.
- *Pasta Sauna*. Commissioned by Performa 09, the third edition of the biennial of new visual art performance in New York City. New York, USA.

Products
- Marshmellow clouds made with rainwater.
- Marshmellow Icebergs to melt in your hot chocolate for inner global warming.

2008
- Solo Exhibition *Eating And Design Part 2: What Design Can Do*, Axis Gallery. Tokyo, Japan.
- Lecture at Design Hotels Future forum. Berlin, Germany.
- Lecture at TCDC (Thailand creative & design center). Bangkok, Thailand.
- *Roots* Installation at Mintshop 10th Anniversary. London, UK.
- Lecture at Folk Futures seminar. Stavanger, Norway.
- Exhibition *Op Je Bord*, selection of works and premiere of *Faked Meat* project at Kasteel Groeneveld. Baarn, NL.
- Lecture and lunch at the Hong Kong Design Centre. Hong Kong, China.
- Lecture and lunch for the Nike design department. Amsterdam, NL.
- Awarded the EDBR-portfolio prize, which is a part of the Rotterdam Design Prize. Awarded by the Economic development board Rotterdam.
- Solo exhibition *Fuel* at showroom MAMA. Rotterdam, NL.
- Lecture and tea for the international Nando's marketing team. Dubai, UAE.
- *Khobz w Melh on the Green Line*, a lecture and workshop with Souk el Tayeb. Beirut, Lebanon.
- Lecture at Design Indaba 11. Capetown, South Africa.
- *Photosynthesistree* installation for FOM (Fundamenteel Onderzoek der Materie / Fundamental Research of Matter). Veldhoven, NL.
- *Burns Night Supper* for Glenmorangie Whisky. London, UK.

Credits

2007
- Lecture for the Nestlé design team. York, UK.
- *Bossche Broekje* cakes in collaboration with Helmut Smits for the CBK (centrum beeldende kunst / centre for visual arts). 's-Hertogenbosch, NL.
- Self initiated chocolate wall, cocoa powder explosion and experiments with chocolate, exhibited at *Chocola d'amour* at Kunsthal. Rotterdam, NL.
- 2-page article for Items magazine about the importance of food as a medium of design.
- *Veggie bling-bling* children's vegetable project for a book 'maak indruk op je kinderen' (impress children) by Snor publishers. NL.
- *Monochrome lunch*, a lunch table for a photo shoot for Wallpaper magazine. London, UK.
- *Trouser factor food*, a food concept for BMW. London, UK.
- *Eating To The Beat*, a composition for the Krossin' Gouda Festival at museumgoudA. Gouda, NL.
- *Sustainability Dinner*, a dinner for the Donck Sessions at Huis then Donck. Ridderkerk, NL.
- *Basics and Accessories*, lunch for the fashion biennale. Arnhem, NL.
- *Dutch Food in Dakar*, a series of bites, based on traditional Dutch food, served on a contemporary way at the Dutch embassy. Dakar, Senegal.
- *Ham Man* installation, traditional Spanish ham tasting, for 'Barcelona 1900' at the Van Gogh Museum. Amsterdam, NL.
- 3 spreads about food and design for Hollands Diep magazine. NL.
- *Dutch National Tapwater Tasting*. A collection of 12 tap waters from all Dutch provinces presented in an empty water basin. Commissioned by KORT, (kunst openbare ruimte Tilburg / art in public space). Tilburg, NL.
- Jury member for the annual HEMA design contest. NL.

2006
- *Connection Dinner* for Droog at Droog@home. Amsterdam, NL.
- Lecture and lunch for the Procter & Gamble design team. Brussels, Belgium.
- Official opening of *Proef* in Amsterdam with a new concept about the apple-harvesting season. Amsterdam, NL.
- *One-minute food* cooking concept for a photo shoot for Food and Wine magazine in collaboration with Marcel Wanders at Proef. Amsterdam, NL.
- *White Funeral Dinner* exhibited at the post mortum exhibition by the Design Academy Eindhoven during the Salone del Mobile. Milan, Italy.
- Lecture for the NII (Nederlands Interieur Instituut / Dutch Interior Institute). Amsterdam, NL.
- Keynote speaker at the Design and Emotion conference. Gothenburg, Sweden.
- Workshop and lecture at the Royal College of Art. London, UK.

2005
- Awarded the 'Ketelbinkie' award for the most innovative enterprise in Rotterdam. The main criteria are that the company has less than 50 employees and represents the city of Rotterdam on a national and international level.
- Workshop during the Semaine folle at art academy L'Esad. Reims, France.
- *Sharing Dinner* for Droog at Droog@home. Amsterdam, NL.
- *Everybody Is An Egg* installation as a part of the exhibition called Dutch mountains, about the new Dutch identity for Her Majesty the Queen at the MU. Eindhoven, NL.
- *Ruis* dinner as part of the theatrical performance 'Ruis' by Powerboat. Rotterdam, NL.
- 3 spreads about food and design for Dutch ELLE magazine.
- *Black Confetti* performance serving original World War II recipes at the historical museum Het Schielandshuis. Rotterdam, NL.
- *Urban Eco Dinner* for Droog and Nike at Droog@home. Amsterdam, NL.
- Serving *Urbatarian* food at the opening of the exhibition of Haunting Dogs Full Of Grace during the Salone del Mobile. Milan, Italy.
- *Contemporary Frysian Food* for the opening of Koninklijke Tichelaar. Makkum, NL.
- Temporary café *Proef het Geluk* at art festival Pursuit of Happiness at Leidse Rijn. Utrecht, NL.

2004
- *Pepperbombs* performance for the opening of Droog@home at the Staalstraat. Amsterdam, NL.
- Food concept for *Go Slow* installation for Droog during the Salone del Mobile. Milan, Italy.
- *Forgotten Vegetables* installation at the Droog exhibition Open borders. Lille, France.
- Opening of *Proef* serving *Elements*. Rotterdam, NL.
- Juni was born!
- *Weeds and Pigeons* for the launch of Codex Kodanski, at the historical museum Het Schielandshuis. Rotterdam, NL.

2003
- *Food Wave* range of snacks for Artotheek Den Haag. The Hague, NL.
- *Butterflies* installation for underwear designer Marlies Dekkers at Museum Boijmans van Beuningen. Rotterdam, NL.
- Edible crockery and root vegetable meal for the opening of the exhibition called *ARMOUR* at a fortress near Asperen for Lidewij Edelkoort. Asperen, NL.
- *Ruik Rotterdam* an installation where visitors were invited to use their noses instead of their eyes to make food choices, at the historical museum Het Schielandshuis. Rotterdam, NL.

2002
- *Colour food* concept for a healthy snack corner at Pediatrics 2000, a pediatrics clinic in New York, USA.

2000
- *Food That Makes You Smell And Taste Good* a series of snacks that influence body odor in collaboration with Floor Cornelisse, commissioned by Ilse Crawford for the Launch of BARE magazine. London, UK.
- Graduation of the Design Academy Eindhoven with a study on 3D knitting and a series of new-traditional Dutch costumes.

1999
- Presentation of the *White Funeral Dinner* during the Salone del Mobile at the first exhibition of the Design Academy Eindhoven. Milan, Italy.

Text: Louise Schouwenberg

Translation: Michael Gibbs

Project Descriptions: Marije Vogelzang

Illustrations: Marije Vogelzang

Graphic Design: Studio Kluif (www.studiokluif.com)

Photography:
- Thomas Pelgrom (www.thomaspelgrom.nl) - Cover
- MAMA - Daniëlle van Ark - p. 14,15,16,17.
- Andreia Costa (www.andreiacosta.nl) - p. 22 bottom, 25, 28, 29 2nd picture, 33, 44, 45, 80, 81 bottom, 104 top, 105 right, 148.
- Piet Hekker - p. 27.
- Bob Eshuis (www.bobeshuis.nl) - p. 32.
- Ingmar Swalue (www.ingmarswalue.com) - p. 34.
- Dik Nicolai (www.diknicolai.com) - p. 48, 49.
- ELLE Wonen
  Photography Inga Powilleit
  Stylist Mirella Sahetapy - p. 72, 73.
- Droog (www.droog.com) - p. 78, 79, 111 2nd and 3rd.
- Yo de Boer - p. 74, 76 2nd and 3rd, 77.
- Glenmorangie Whisky - p. 88, 89 bottom.
- Joost van de Weghe - p. 96, 97.
- John Dummer - p. 122.
- Annie Collinge for Icon Issue 059 May 2008 - p. 157.
- Alan Jensen - p. 26, 27, 28, 29.
- Kenji Masunaga - p. 4
- Willem van den Heuvel - p. 5

Proef
Gosschalklaan 12
1014DC Amsterdam
The Netherlands
www.proefamsterdam.nl
info@proefamsterdam.nl

Studio Marije Vogelzang - www.marijevogelzang.nl

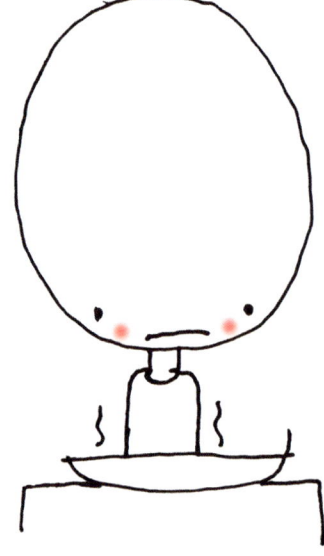